A Voluntary Tax?

Studies of Government Finance: Second Series

TITLES PUBLISHED

A Voluntary Tax?

*New Perspectives
on Sophisticated Estate Tax
Avoidance*

GEORGE COOPER

Studies of Government Finance

THE BROOKINGS INSTITUTION

WASHINGTON, D.C.

Library of Congress Cataloging in Publication Data:

Cooper, George, 1937–
  A voluntary tax?: New perspectives on sophisticated estate tax avoidance
  (Studies of government finance: Second series)
  Includes bibliographical references and index.
  1. Inheritance and transfer tax—United States.   2. Estate planning—
United States.   I. Title.   II. Series.
KF6584.C66   343.73′053   78-20853
ISBN 0-8157-1552-8
ISBN 0-8157-1551-X pbk.

9 8 7 6 5 4 3 2 1

THE BROOKINGS INSTITUTION is an independent organization devoted to nonpartisan research, education, and publication in economics, government, foreign policy, and the social sciences generally. Its principal purposes are to aid in the development of sound public policies and to promote public understanding of issues of national importance.

The Institution was founded on December 8, 1927, to merge the activities of the Institute for Government Research, founded in 1916, the Institute of Economics, founded in 1922, and the Robert Brookings Graduate School of Economics and Government, founded in 1924.

The Board of Trustees is responsible for the general administration of the Institution, while the immediate direction of the policies, program, and staff is vested in the President, assisted by an advisory committee of the officers and staff. The by-laws of the Institution state: "It is the function of the Trustees to make possible the conduct of scientific research, and publication, under the most favorable conditions, and to safeguard the independence of the research staff in the pursuit of their studies and in the publication of the results of such studies. It is not a part of their function to determine, control, or influence the conduct of particular investigations or the conclusions reached."

The President bears final responsibility for the decision to publish a manuscript as a Brookings book. In reaching his judgment on the competence, accuracy, and objectivity of each study, the President is advised by the director of the appropriate research program and weighs the views of a panel of expert outside readers who report to him in confidence on the quality of the work. Publication of a work signifies that it is deemed a competent treatment worthy of public consideration but does not imply endorsement of conclusions or recommendations.

The Institution maintains its position of neutrality on issues of public policy in order to safeguard the intellectual freedom of the staff. Hence interpretations or conclusions in Brookings publications should be understood to be solely those of the authors and should not be attributed to the Institution, to its trustees, officers, or other staff members, or to the organizations that support its research.

Foreword

THE DISTRIBUTION of wealth in the United States has changed very little over the past several decades. A series of Brookings studies has explored the importance of inheritance as a source of individual wealth holdings through inference from statistical data sources. What these studies fail to explain, however, is why material inheritance remains influential in a society with extremely high estate and gift taxes. Have these taxes, whose rates have been as high as 77 percent for most of the past generation, seriously interfered with the intergenerational transfer of substantial wealth?

This study, by a Columbia University law professor trained in the arcane art of estate tax practice, addresses that question. George Cooper, writing as a member of the Brookings associated staff, draws not only upon his own knowledge and the published literature but also upon court records and interviews with estate planners. He explains how sophisticated estate planning can be used to avoid the estate tax, and he illustrates this process with a number of case studies.

Cooper notes that federal estate and gift taxes now apply only to some 1 or 2 percent of the population. He concludes that the effect of the estate tax "is more cosmetic than real and the economy is paying the price of fettered capital and distorted property ownership for this cosmetology." He discusses alternative methods of accomplishing the same goals without the economic distortions, noting that his sometimes controversial proposals are "intended to provoke consideration of further reform, more than to determine what the reform should be."

This study was originally published as an article in the March 1977 issue of the *Columbia Law Review*. For its republication as a Brookings book, the author changed it to reflect the Revenue Act of 1978. He acknowledges the help of the many estate planners who cooperated in sharing their ideas with him. He is also grateful for the research assistance of Terence Kinsman. Florence Robinson prepared the index.

The project was supported by a grant from the Ford Foundation. This is the ninth publication in the second series of Brookings Studies of Government Finance. Both series are devoted to examining issues in taxation and public expenditure policy. The views expressed in this volume are the author's alone and should not be ascribed to the Ford Foundation, or to the officers, trustees, or other staff members of the Brookings Institution.

BRUCE K. MACLAURY
President

November 1978
Washington, D.C.

Contents

Introduction

In fact, we haven't got an estate tax, what we have, you pay an estate tax if you want to; if you don't want to, you don't have to.[1]

WHEN WILLIAM DU PONT, JR., great-grandson of the founder of E. I. du Pont de Nemours & Company, died in 1965, each of his five children received an inheritance of more than $50 million. Each will receive an additional sum, worth more than $40 million at 1966 values, on the death of their aunt, Marion du Pont Scott, who is now 84 years old. Thus these five individuals are the sole inheritors of an aggregate family fortune worth almost a half billion dollars in 1966. Yet the total of all estate and gift taxes—including taxes payable on the aunt's death—from the origins of the fortune in nineteenth century du Pont Company profits until receipt by the present generation, will be less than $25 million. Two generations will have died while estate taxes were in effect, giving a combined effective tax rate of 5 percent for both generations.

The first purpose of this book is to explain how a phenomenon of this nature occurred despite an estate tax with rates as high as 77 percent on wealth over $10 million, backed up by a gift tax with rates to

1. *Estate and Gift Taxes: Hearings Before the House Ways and Means Comm.*, 94th Cong., 2d Sess., pt. 2, 1335 (March 15-23, 1976) (Statement of Prof. A. James Casner) [hereinafter cited as *Hearings*]. This comment was directed at the situation before the Tax Reform Act of 1976, notably use of generation-skipping trusts. Whether it remains true today is a question examined in this book.

57.75 percent on such fortunes.[2] The second purpose is to explore whether the current generation can continue this pattern of tax avoidance in light of the major estate and gift tax reforms enacted by Congress in 1976.[3] The perhaps surprising conclusion compelled by our findings is that today's multimillionaires, as well as persons of lesser wealth, need pay a stiff estate and gift tax no more than did their predecessors. It may be that the real certainties of this world are death and tax *avoidance*.

These findings are based on an extensive review of judicial decisions and the published literature in the field of estate planning, additional research in court files to obtain information not available in the published record, and a series of interviews with several dozen lawyers and certified public accountants who specialize in the subject. While the group interviewed was by no means a research sample, it was broad and diverse enough to give us a good sense of the situation and to enable us to reach useful conclusions about the

2. These rates were in effect from 1941 to 1976 for the estate tax and from 1942 to 1976 for the gift tax. *See Hearings, supra* note 1, at 1212 (statement of Richard B. Covey); W. WARREN & S. SURREY, FEDERAL ESTATE AND GIFT TAXATION: CASES AND MATERIALS (1961 ed.). Under the new single rate scale for gifts and bequests provided by the Tax Reform Act of 1976, Pub. L. 94-455, 90 Stat. 1888, the maximum rate is 70% on transfers in excess of $5,000,000. *See* new I.R.C. § 2001(c). (All section references in this book are to the Internal Revenue Code of 1954, *as amended*. The term "new" is used where appropriate to designate a provision added by the Tax Reform Act of 1976, and the term "old" to designate a provision deleted by that Act.)

3. The Tax Reform Act of 1976 made several major changes in the general pattern of estate and gift taxation. The basic levels of exemption under these taxes have been doubled, effectively reducing the portion of the population subject to the taxes from 6%-7% to 1%-2%. *See* ch. 1, note 11 and accompanying text *infra*. For those who remain subject to the taxes, however, they have been stiffened, most notably in the following respects: (1) Gifts, which were formerly taxed on a separate rate scale and at three-quarters the rates of bequests, are now taxed under a single combined rate scale with bequests—the bequests, in effect, being treated as the ultimate gift. *See* ch. 2 text accompanying note 2 *infra*. (2) Generation-skipping transfers are now subject to a special supplementary tax designed to impose essentially the same burden as if the intervening generation(s) had held property outright. *See* ch. 2 text accompanying notes 125-29 *infra*. (3) Heirs, who formerly took all inherited property with a stepped-up basis equal to the death value of the property, now get a stepped-up basis only with respect to appreciation before 1976; as to post-1976 appreciation, they take a carryover basis equal to the decedent's basis; but this applies only to persons dying after 1979. *See* ch. 1 text accompanying note 13 *infra*. The 1976 Act also made a number of other changes of narrower significance, many of which will be referred to where relevant in this book.

current status of tax techniques in estate planning and the potential for expansion and development of those techniques in the future. In other words, it is not possible on the basis of our research to quantify the significance of any particular technique, nor can we say that we know every last trick in the estate planner's book. We can say with some confidence, however, that we have a reasonable idea of the range of approaches that might be taken by estate planners in handling various types of estates and that we are probably aware of most major techniques now in common use.[4]

This study is presented in four chapters. Chapter 1 provides an overview of our findings. Chapter 2 discusses in detail the most important planning techniques. Chapter 3 gives examples of actual cases where these techniques have been used to good advantage and shows how these techniques were or might be combined effectively to reduce transfer taxes in particular cases. A detailed discussion of the du Pont situation mentioned above is included, with specifics of a hypothetical estate plan that would totally avoid tax on the current generation. Finally, chapter 4 offers some proposals and suggestions for reform.

4. One group of interviewees, constituting approximately two-thirds of the total, was carefully selected on the basis of informed recommendations with a view to locating a group of the highest level, most sophisticated, planners. The other third was chosen from lists of persons who had indicated a special interest in estate and gift taxation through bar association committee membership or similar organizational affiliation. In addition to our initial interviews with these practitioners, we later held a follow-up conference attended by several of the most knowledgeable to review a draft of this study and circulated that draft for comments to all others. The draft was also reviewed with experienced Internal Revenue Service estate auditors. The persons interviewed had a variety of clients ranging from those with very large amounts of inherited wealth to those with smaller and more recently acquired fortunes and came from a variety of practice situations, including large general practice firms and smaller firms specializing in tax matters. The interviewees were located in three different cities, New York, Washington, and Atlanta, enabling us to get some feel for regional disparities in planning.

To encourage candor, we advised all interviewees that they would not be quoted by name and that pledge is adhered to throughout this book. Since, as explained later, our method is for the most part to describe what *can* be done, rather than what one individual planner did, and since we have independently determined the legal status of all planning suggestions with our own research, we believe this absence of individual names poses no problem. A list of all persons interviewed is on file with the *Columbia Law Review*. Most of these persons were seen by the author, and the others by research assistants, Toni Robinson and G. Warren Whitaker, who provided valuable assistance.

CHAPTER ONE

Overview

IT IS DIFFICULT TO AVOID the general conclusion that the present estate and gift tax base is already seriously eroded and could be entirely washed away if taxpayers put a strong effort into doing so. The fact that any substantial amount of tax is now being collected can be attributed only to taxpayer indifference to avoidance opportunities or a lack of aggressiveness on the part of estate planners in exploiting the loopholes that exist. A leading expert at recent Ways and Means Committee hearings was not hyperbolizing when he offered the comment quoted at the head of this book. For those who do not want to contribute their estates to the government (or to charity), there is an impressive array of strategies for moving wealth from one generation to another outside the purview of estate and gift taxation. Most of this remains largely untouched by the Tax Reform Act of 1976.

Despite the myriad of variations, sophisticated estate tax avoidance can be categorized according to three basic themes. First, the technique of estate freezing keeps free of tax the future growth in an individual's wealth by diverting that growth to the next generation. Second, the creation of tax-exempt wealth takes advantage of special provisions in the tax code that exempt certain assets from taxation.

Finally, the reduction or elimination of tax on existing wealth is made possible by a package of techniques for gift-giving, manipulating valuations and exploiting charitable deductions. All these basic themes are well known to estate planners, although everyone is, of course, not familiar with the details of every variation.

There is, however, a surprising gap between the knowledge of techniques and the actual use of them. Some categories, such as use of loan guarantees to provide a tax-free capital base for the next generation and diversions of business opportunities to that generation, do not appear to be often recommended or used by estate planners. This does not mean that these techniques are not much in evidence. To the contrary, there is a general consensus that use of such measures by clients on their own, without consulting an estate planner or even consciously engaging in estate planning, is widespread. The same is true of providing children with inside information and of other approaches for giving prospective heirs the informal benefit of parental knowledge, talent, and capital. The simple fact is that much transfer tax avoidance is more the by-product of human nature than part of estate planning. It is normal for parents to assist their children, and the line between a gift of parental advice and one of a business opportunity is exceedingly fine. Many, if not most, of the situations in which a parent provides lifetime economic benefits to his children are probably not thought of as requiring consultation with a lawyer. Who sees his estate planner before cosigning his son's note at the bank? This observation does not detract from the importance of these techniques as tax reduction devices. However, it does give warning of the major practical problems in line-drawing and implementation that must be faced if any transfer tax is to be made truly comprehensive. We return to this problem in chapter 4.

There remains a large area of estate planning where self-help is not practicable. This is the province of the estate planner but even here there is no apparent uniformity in use of techniques, even those most widely known. For example, the preferred stock recapitalization (described in detail shortly) as a technique to pass on future growth in a closely held corporation is old hat to estate planners.[1] Everyone

1. *See, e.g.*, Williams, *Using a Recapitalization to Reallocate Equity Interests and Perpetuate Closely Held Status*, 32 N.Y.U. INST. FED. TAX. 715, 720-29 (1974); Ehrlich, *Corporate Recapitalization as an Estate Planning Business Retention Tool,*

knows it well and seems to understand its advantages and disadvantages. But the frequency of its use is quite a different matter.
Some interviewees said that they used it several times a year, while
others said that they had never used it in many years of practice.
Several factors cause such disparities in use:

1. *Levels of legal sophistication.* It is one thing to know about a
technique and something very different to be willing and able to
implement it. A procedure such as the preferred stock recapitalization is fraught with technical difficulties, which could frighten off
many planners. This is a finding of some significance, because all of
the persons interviewed were chosen for their known interest in estate
and gift taxation. If persons in this group are bothered by technical
complexity, it may mean that a technique is beyond the ken of other
lawyers. Of course this complexity problem erodes over time, as a
technique becomes more commonly used and discussed, but it surely
is a serious deterrent to widespread use of newer devices. For example, the rules governing charitable split-interest trusts (trusts in
which beneficial interests are divided between charitable and noncharitable beneficiaries) are so recondite that one interviewee was
willing to wager that no one who attempted to set up such a trust
without substantial experience in the area could avoid making some
fatal error. Yet these trusts are immensely important planning tools,
as we shall see.

2. *Differences among clients' attitudes.* The interviewees described their clients' attitudes toward estate planning in surprisingly
diverse terms. Some said that clients had little or no interest in aggressive planning for tax saving. This group suggested that their
clients' planning interests were in the nontax area—such as assuring
that their widows would be adequately provided for—and that they
were uninterested in pursuing estate planning beyond the extent
necessary to accomplish that goal. The idea of preserving a fortune
as such, or of avoiding estate taxes for the mere sake of doing so, was
not a major client consideration in the opinion of these interviewees.
Several planners described careful tax-saving procedures they had
developed and held in readiness for clients but which clients refused
to adopt. Others spoke, in tones ranging from frustration to bemuse-

---

34 N.Y.U. Inst. Fed. Tax. 1661, 1662 (1976). *See also* text, ch. 2, accompanying
notes 3-16 *infra.*

ment to awe, of clients with tens of millions of dollars who refused to pay any attention to the estate tax.[2] Another group of interviewees painted a drastically different picture. In the words of one lawyer, his clients would "stand on one ear, wiggle four toes, and disavow their families to save $20 in tax." The norm is unquestionably somewhere between these extremes, but no one should underestimate the importance of client reluctance as a factor deterring more enterprising estate planning. There is certainly a significant group of clients who are ambivalent about transfer tax saving or, at least, accord it a low priority. Saving estate taxes apparently does not generate the same high level of enthusiasm as saving income taxes, for the obvious reason that the benefits to the client from estate tax avoidance are much more indirect and intangible. In addition, the natural reluctance to undertake elaborate preparations for death should not be ignored as an inhibiting factor.[3]

3. *Evaluation of nonestate and gift tax factors.* All of the techniques available for avoiding estate and gift taxes have some byproducts. The income tax considerations are important and often conflict with transfer tax objectives. For example, most transfer tax avoidance techniques necessarily involve a shift of property to the successor generation without passing the property through a taxable estate. This sacrifices the opportunity for use of step-up of basis with resulting capital gains tax avoidance, which was a critical income tax avoidance strategy before basis rules were modified by the Tax Reform Act of 1976.[4]

Even more important are the nontax considerations. It is necessary under many transfer tax techniques to pass some rights and ownership to children in advance of a parent's death, a result that is often undesired. The loss of self resulting from property transfers is a littleexplored psychological and philosophical issue but is no doubt a serious matter for those who believe "I am what I have."[5] The children's rights can be kept to a minimum, and the parent's continuing

2. An extreme example was the case of a client with a $50-$60 million estate who, with an air of *noblesse oblige,* told his lawyer that he did not want to avoid high death taxes because they were a desirable social phenomenon to reassure the public that entrenched wealth was not dominating the country.

3. *See generally* T. SHAFFER, DEATH, PROPERTY AND LAWYERS chs. 1, 4, 5 (1970).

4. *See* text accompanying note 13 *infra.*

5. J. P. Sartre, *quoted in* T. SHAFFER, *supra* note 3, at 8. *See id.* at 4-8.

control maximized, through use of corporate and trust devices, but those devices burden property with ownership complexity which many persons wish to avoid. Another nontax problem is the need to find suitable recipients of property. Given the well-known difficulties of retaining property ownership after death, it is necessary for the tax avoider to identify specific heirs or beneficiaries to whom property ownership can be diverted. The wealthy person, such as Howard Hughes, who cannot easily identify these successors faces a rather serious estate-planning dilemma.

In many instances, these offsetting problems may be enough to nullify an estate planning proposal. In other cases, they may simply give added cause for indecision—in an area where there is already a natural human tendency to waver—and lead to a delay in estate planning until it is too late to undertake many of the most effective measures.

4. *Differences in the size and composition of estates.* Many of the more sophisticated estate planning techniques are simply not worth the effort except in the case of ultralarge estates. Others are applicable only where certain kinds of assets, such as a closely held business, are present. Some estate planners tend to have more clients who fall into these categories than others. It should not be thought, however, that this factor is always controlling, since many lawyers who had clients in situations which seemingly suggested a particular planning technique did not make use of the technique for some other reason.

5. *Diverse styles among estate planners.* The persons interviewed varied from those who obviously believed strongly in aggressive transfer tax avoidance and who sold that idea to their clients to those who took a more passive role. It is also obvious that there is a range in the level of rapport between client and lawyer, which greatly influences the extent to which a lawyer's more elaborate planning suggestions will be embraced by a client.

6. *Peer custom and practice.* Lawyers talk to each other and so do wealthy clients. The expectable result is that the choice of planning techniques varies, as one interviewee put it, "like fad and fashion." A good example of this is that one particularly effective use of charitable split-interest trusts is unheard of in either Washington or Atlanta (and is mentioned only obliquely in the literature) but is all the rage among top-level New York planners. On the other hand, certain in-

stallment sale techniques that are known but rarely used in New York are among the most popular and most-used procedures in Atlanta.[6] These regional variations are not necessarily irrational. For instance, the use of installment sales in Atlanta seems to have been provoked by a favorable decision in the Fifth Circuit Court of Appeals.[7] However, rational or not, it is clear that there are trends in estate planning, which vary from time to time and place to place.

For all these reasons, it is not possible even to venture a guess on the precise amount of estate and gift tax avoidance that results from the use of the techniques discussed in this book. A few important conclusions can be drawn, nonetheless. First, the amounts involved are probably not overwhelming in terms of overall federal revenues. The amount produced by current estate and gift taxation is so small that even a doubling of revenues from this source, a not unreasonable expectation, would produce only a 1 or 2 percent increase in overall federal tax collections. This does not mean that the revenue potential is to be ignored. Based on the facts involved in the handful of cases discussed in this book, one may fairly surmise that hundreds of millions and possibly many billions of dollars of revenue are lost to the federal treasury because of taxpayer exploitation of the opportunities described. A sum of this magnitude is worth thinking about in revenue terms even if it is dwarfed by the gargantuan federal budget.

This is not the only reason, however, for being concerned about these matters. It is plain that, whatever the revenue implications, the techniques discussed drastically undercut the other generally stated objectives of the estate and gift tax. These objectives are variously described as breaking up large concentrations of wealth,[8] limiting the extent to which wealthy parents can confer unearned advantages on their children,[9] and providing a backup for the income tax, which

6. One interviewee who had recently spoken on the same topic at estate planning conferences in New York and Atlanta had asked for a show of hands in each city by all who had used a particular estate planning device (the private annuity). There was a barely noticeable showing in New York and a forest of hands in Atlanta.

7. Rushing v. Commissioner, 441 F.2d 593 (5th Cir. 1971).

8. *See* President F. D. Roosevelt's Message to Congress on Tax Methods and Policy, H.R. Doc. No. 229, 74th Cong., 1st Sess. (June 19, 1935); C. Shoup, Federal Estate and Gift Taxes 100-01, 119-20 (1966).

9. *Hearings, supra* Intro. note 1, at 1210 (statement of Richard B. Covey); 17 Works of Theodore Roosevelt 504-05 (Mem. ed. 1925); C. Shoup, *supra* note 8, at 100-01, 119-20.

will check avoidance of it and provide an additional element of progressivity in the tax system.[10] The examples in the pages that follow raise serious questions about how well those goals are being accomplished.

In addition, as with any tax, the estate and gift tax should operate evenhandedly, taxing similarly situated people alike and avoiding unintended incentives to distort behavior for tax-saving purposes. The estate and gift tax clearly is not working in that way. The tax burden on any individual depends as much on the form in which he or she holds assets and the special planning steps that have been taken with regard to those assets as on the total value of asset holdings. This obvious loss of equity and neutrality must be a matter of serious concern.

There is good reason to believe that the problems described here will grow in importance if corrective action is not taken. More than one interviewee warned that he sensed a growing client interest in estate and gift tax avoidance. To the extent that this interest develops it will offset the client reluctance, which is today such an important factor in restraining the aggressive exploitation of avoidance opportunities.

A brief examination of the likely effects of the Tax Reform Act of 1976 reinforces the prognosis that interest in estate tax avoidance will grow. The Act, by increasing the basic estate tax-exempt levels to $175,000 for single persons (up from $60,000) and to $425,000 for married persons (up from $120,000),[11] will relieve much of the developing pressure from persons of modest wealth for estate tax avoidance. But insofar as it also closes off some popular tax reduction possibilities available to the very wealthy (primarily the opportunities for low-rate taxation of gifts and use of generation-skipping trusts),[12] the legislation gives renewed emphasis to avoidance-seek-

10. *Hearings, supra* Intro. note 1, at 1236 (statement of Michael J. Graetz); Surrey, *An Introduction to Revision of the Federal Estate and Gift Taxes,* 38 CALIF. L. REV. 1, 6 (1950).

11. *See* new I.R.C. §§ 2001, 2010, 2056(c)(1)(A). The 1976 Act does not contain an exemption as such but rather a credit, which offsets the tax on a set amount of property. The figures in text refer to the amounts so offset. These figures are rounded and represent the exemption levels as of 1981, when the Act will be fully phased in. All computations in this book for post-1976 law take account of the fully phased-in exemptions.

12. These two aspects of present law are estimated by Gerald Jantscher to have

ing by that group. It certainly will force a review of all estate plans and generate a natural momentum on the part of those adversely affected by it to pursue aggressively new avoidance mechanisms that are unaffected by the legislative reforms, a category into which most of the devices discussed in this book fall. Because of the existence of these alternatives, one experienced estate planner suggested that the reforms will simply create a "churning" in estate plans, as clients move to use new avoidance techniques, but little real change in the burdens of taxation on the very wealthy.

One other aspect of the 1976 Act, while not technically a change in estate and gift taxation, is likely to increase greatly interest in estate tax avoidance. This is the income tax law change that erodes the opportunity to hold appreciated property until death and pass on the property free of capital gains tax. For all decedents dying after 1979, the heirs will now carry over basis and pay capital gains tax when they sell property as to all post-1976 appreciation, although they will continue to escape capital gains tax on pre-1976 appreciation.[13] The effect of this change, from the viewpoint of estate taxation, is to remove one of the major disincentives to estate tax avoidance. Under the old rule, there was a great advantage in submitting property to the estate tax because only in that fashion could the reward of a step-up in basis be obtained. Under the new law, this compensating reward has been withdrawn and we may expect to see many persons undertaking estate tax avoidance who were formerly deterred from doing so for fear of losing the chance to use step-up in basis. The impact of this change will be gradual as the relative importance of pre-1976 appreciation diminishes over time.

Since it would be premature even to attempt prediction of precisely what will happen in response to the 1976 Act, this book focuses on what has been done and what can be done by at least a significant segment of estate planners, on the assumption that much of this will be done with increasing frequency unless the law is somehow further modified to restrain it.

---

cost $1.15 billion in revenue in the fiscal year 1977. *See* Letter from Gerald Jantscher to Prof. Paul P. McDaniel (May 18, 1976).

13. *See* new I.R.C. § 1023, as amended by Revenue Act of 1978.

CHAPTER TWO

Current Planning Techniques

ESTATE-PLANNING TECHNIQUES fall into three categories: freezing the estate, creating tax-exempt wealth, and disposing of wealth already accumulated.

Freezing the Estate

The first major goal of good estate planning is to freeze the size of a client's estate at its current level and divert future growth to the natural objects of the client's bounty. As will be seen, it is far easier to divert future growth than it is to disgorge wealth already accumulated, and good estate planning attempts to get estate-freezing action into operation as soon as possible so as to cut off wealth accumulation before it becomes a more serious planning problem. The most straightforward technique for accomplishing this is simply for the client to give large portions of his property to his children. This procedure shifts the future potential of that property to the children, and under pre-1976 law took advantage of the fact that lifetime gifts were taxed at relatively favorable rates. But even under old law this straightforward approach had serious drawbacks. It required payment of an immediate gift tax which could have become a substantial sum if large amounts were being transferred,[1] and it caused a loss of control over property, which ran counter to the natural inclination of many wealthy persons. For these reasons, the client who relied on simple gifts engaged only in what might be called low-level estate planning. He merely took advantage of opportunities which the law held out for the taking and, indeed, may have been doing only what the law sought to induce.

The disadvantages of straightforward gift-giving have been substantially aggravated by the Tax Reform Act. The gift tax has now been unified with the estate tax, so that the two function as a single combined tax with one rate scale and the relative tax rate advantages of gifts over bequests have been drastically reduced. Some advantage remains in lifetime gift-giving because the tax is imposed only on the net amount actually given, while the estate tax base includes amounts used to pay the tax as well as sums actually received by heirs. This benefit, while substantial, is offset by the fact that the tax on a lifetime gift must be paid immediately rather than deferred until death and, in any event, is relatively insignificant compared to that available before 1976. The burdens of a gift tax thus loom as a much more serious problem now than before the Reform Act.[2]

Therefore, it has always been worthwhile, and is now virtually essential, for the superior estate planner to recommend more than simple straightforward gift-giving. Where the estate planner has traditionally earned his fee is in accomplishing one or more of three sophisticated goals in gift-giving—continuing control of and benefits from the transferred property in the hands of the client, reducing or avoiding the need to pay immediate gift tax on the transfer, and passing on more of value than meets the eye in the transfer. All this has been and remains possible for anyone willing to maneuver enough to achieve it.

The Preferred Stock Recapitalization

Take the case of Dr. Joseph E. Salsbury.[3] Dr. Salsbury was the founder and developer of Salsbury Laboratories, a company produc-

1. For example, under old law the gift tax rate hit 29.25% at $1,000,000 and 50.25% at $5,000,000. Old I.R.C. § 2502.

2. The new tax rates for donative transfers, whether by gift or bequest, hit 41% at $1,000,000 and 70% at $5,000,000. New I.R.C. § 2001(c).

3. Estate of Joseph E. Salsbury, 34 T.C.M. (CCH) 1441 (1975). The discussion

ing drug and health products for the poultry industry. The company was begun on a shoestring in 1927, but by the time of Dr. Salsbury's death in 1967 it had worldwide sales of $14.9 million and was conservatively valued by the Tax Court at more than $13 million. Dr. Salsbury personally continued to have complete voting control over the corporation and no one other than he and the natural objects of his bounty owned any interest in it. Yet, thanks to good estate planning years earlier, Dr. Salsbury paid little gift tax and his estate was taxed on only a small fraction of corporate value.

Dr. Salsbury's estate planning began sometime before 1946. By that year, almost two decades after the corporation's founding in 1927, he had transferred 46 percent of its single class of stock to his wife and two children, directly and in trust. The record in the case does not indicate how or when Mrs. Salsbury and the children acquired their shares, but the shares must have been given by Dr. Salsbury at some time between 1927 and 1946. We do not know how much gift tax was paid when these shares were transferred, but because the corporation was surely worth much less in these earlier years and because the gifts were divided among three persons and may have been spread over many years, the tax was probably small if not nonexistent.[4] Thus, even if no estate planning had been done after 1946, Dr. Salsbury would have been no slouch at the planning process. He would have succeeded in shifting several million dollars of corporate value to his wife and children with little or no estate or gift tax liability.

Moreover, this would not have been simple, low-level estate planning. By retaining majority voting control in the corporation, Dr. Salsbury effectively continued in control of the property he gave to his prospective heirs. He continued to have the power to select all

---

in the text is based on the facts reported by the court as supplemented by data in the full record on file at the Tax Court.

4. The conclusion that little gift tax was paid on transfer of shares from Dr. Joseph Salsbury to his wife and children is supported by other data in the record. This shows that subsequently, between 1943 and 1955, John and Frances Salsbury, the children of Dr. Joseph, transferred 9,053 shares of common stock (32% of the total) giving a total value of $520,323 and paying a total gift tax of only $96,149. Most of these transfers took place in 1955, when the stock was probably worth substantially more than in the pre-1946 period when the transfers from Dr. Salsbury occurred. Furthermore, it is even possible that all or a portion of Dr. Salsbury's transfers were made at a time before 1932, when there was no gift tax in effect.

corporate directors and, through them, to choose all the officers who ran the corporation, to fix the salaries of all officers, and to decide when and how much to pay in dividends. This continued control over property through retained voting control of a corporation is not viewed as continuing ownership for the purpose of the estate tax. In addition, since he continued to run the corporation, Dr. Salsbury also achieved the goal of giving his prospective heirs the indirect benefit of a portion of his knowledge and talent free of tax insofar as those personal attributes were used to operate and expand the company.

Because the advantages of gifting a minority interest in a closely held corporation in this fashion are so manifold and the process is so simple, it is an immensely popular procedure. Several interviewees told us that they often found it necessary to go no further than this to gain all the estate planning benefit their clients desired.

Dr. Salsbury wished to go further, however. He could have continued the pattern of making gifts and reserving the voting power of the stock to himself to keep control when his personal stock ownership dipped below 50 percent. However, the corporation was growing in value and these additional gifts could have generated a heavy gift tax liability, even under pre-1976 rates, particularly because the earlier gifts might have used up Dr. Salsbury's gift tax exemptions and moved him into higher brackets. We can only speculate on this.

In any event, in 1946 Dr. Salsbury moved on to a new level of sophistication in his estate planning by undertaking a tax-free stock recapitalization, a technique that has in recent years become one of the most powerful weapons in the estate planner's arsenal. Pursuant to this recapitalization, all of Salsbury Laboratories' single class of common stock was canceled, and in place thereof shareholders were issued a combination of new preferred stock and common stock.[5] For dividend purposes, the preferred stock was entitled to a limited payment ($0.06 per share), and all dividends beyond that went to the new common stock. For voting purposes, both preferred and common stock had one vote per share, but since 690,000 shares of preferred were issued and only 27,920 shares of common, it was clear that the preferred shares dominated the vote. The preferred stock

5. The new preferred was designated "Class A common" and the new common was designated "Class B common." There was also a third class of stock designated "preferred" which is unimportant to this discussion.

was divided among shareholders in proportion to their prior holdings of the old common stock, giving Dr. Salsbury 54 percent of it. The new common stock was, however, issued almost entirely to Mrs. Salsbury and the children, Dr. Salsbury taking only a nominal portion (0.6%) for himself.

The net effect on voting rights of this recapitalization was minimal; Dr. Salsbury's control was preserved (slightly reduced to 52 percent). Beyond that, while the facts in the record do not speak to the matter, it may fairly be assumed that this recapitalization followed standard patterns. If these patterns were followed, the aggregate value of the preferred stock was approximately equal to the then value of the corporation,[6] and the new common stock had negligible value, embodying only the speculative future potential of the corporation. On this assumption, Dr. Salsbury had no gift tax to pay,[7] but he had successfully shifted to his wife and children the full value of all future corporate growth. In other words, he froze his own estate, and, at the same time, achieved the triple goals of sophisticated estate planning—no loss of control, no current gift tax, and ability to pass on the future benefits of his business acumen free of tax. Moreover, since he retained voting control in the corporation he had the power to decide how much benefit the common shareholders received and when they received it. They in fact received nothing for eight years —until 1954, when regular dividends on the common stock commenced.

The ultimate result of all of this was that when he died in 1967, although Dr. Salsbury had paid little or no gift tax and in fact continued to hold voting control of the $13 million company he had founded, he actually owned only a limited preferred stock interest that could be included in his estate. This preferred stock was worth, apart from its voting control, only $372,152. The Internal Revenue Service attempted to salvage the situation by arguing that the value of the retained voting control was equal to most of the corporate value, but the Tax Court was unsympathetic and raised the value only modestly to $514,000. The balance of some $12.5 million escaped tax, saving Dr. Salsbury's heirs a potential liability of approximately

6. *See* Burch & Hemmerling, *Estate Planning in an Inflation Economy*, 27 U.S.C. Tax Inst. 489, 504-08 (1975).

7. *Cf.* Rev. Rul. 74-269, 1974-1 C.B. 87 (exchange of common for equal value preferred treated as tax-free reorganization).

$7 million. This effectively allowed the business, which was the only substantial asset owned by Dr. Salsbury, to be passed on to the next generation without any meaningful tax burden.[8]

Had the provisions of the Tax Reform Act applied to Dr. Salsbury, they would have made virtually no difference. The Act does contain a provision treating transfers of corporate stock with retained vote in that stock itself as ineffective for estate tax purposes,[9] and thus restrains an extreme opportunity for retained control permitted under prior law.[10] However, this provision would not seem to have any effect on situations where control is maintained through other shares, as in *Salsbury*. It is true that under the new law Dr. Salsbury's gifts of stock before 1946 would potentially have been subject to higher rates of tax, but they would also have been eligible for the higher basic exemptions now available. As best we can tell, the aggregate value of the gifts before 1946 was less than the basic exemption available to a married man like Dr. Salsbury.[11] As for the stock given in the 1946 recapitalization, that stock had no value (assuming it adhered to the normal pattern for such recapitalizations) and would have been just as free of tax under the new law as it was under the old. Thus the *Salsbury* pattern could be repeated today or any time in the foreseeable future, with essentially the same facts. Indeed, as noted earlier, since future Dr. Salsburys are less likely to be seduced away

8. In fairness to the Salsburys it should be noted that the son took over operation of the business sometime before his father's death and a portion of the $13 million death value was therefore produced by the son. The estate tax avoidance does not depend on this fact, however. The identical estate and gift tax result would have occurred if no child of Dr. Salsbury had ever set foot in Salsbury Laboratories.

9. *See* new I.R.C. § 2036 (b), as modified by Revenue Act of 1978.

10. *E.g.*, United States v. Byrum, 408 U.S. 125 (1972) (retention of voting rights in stock given to trust held not grounds for inclusion of trusted stock in estate); Estate of Gilman, 65 T.C. 296 (1975) (shares held excludable from estate although decedent served as one of three trustees controlling donated shares and was chief executive officer and director of company). *See* Ehrlich, *supra* ch. 1 note 1, at 1677-78; Moore, *Byrum Revisited*, 27 U.S.C. Tax Inst. 439 (1975); Pressment, *Effect of Tax Court's Gilman Decision on Estate Planning for the Close Corporation*, 44 J. Tax 160 (1976).

11. This exemption in the case of lifetime gifts is now $275,625, as compared to $60,000 under prior law. *Compare* new I.R.C. §§ 2505, 2523 *with* old I.R.C. §§ 2521, 2523. Because the workings of the marital deduction for the estate tax are somewhat different than for the gift tax, under new law as well as old, these basic exempt amounts are lower than the comparable estate tax amounts mentioned in the text, ch. 1, at note 12 *supra*.

from such schemes and into holding stock until their death by the siren call of step-up in basis, and because the higher tax rates on gifts will generate new pressure to make large transfers in a tax-free format, the *Salsbury*-type recapitalization is even more likely to be used after the Tax Reform Act than before.

Setting up a recapitalization such as this is not, of course, child's play. In particular, care must be taken in fixing the terms and conditions of the preferred stock to establish its value equal to the then value of the corporation. While these recapitalizations are widely used and referred to, there is surprisingly little in-depth analysis of them in the literature,[12] and there is a consequent wide divergence of opinion among practitioners as to the best strategies for determining such things as the liquidating value and dividend payout on the preferred stock. However, as some of our informants pointed out, there is not all that much risk involved, particularly after the *Salsbury* decision. At most a small gift tax may have to be paid on audit of a gift tax return for the year in which the common stock is given to prospective heirs, and there is a good chance that there will not even be an audit.[13]

A more serious drawback to a preferred stock recapitalization, and the only significant reason given by any of our interviewees for not undertaking one in almost every closely held corporation situation (other than client indifference or reluctance to get involved in tax

12. The best discussions are in Burch & Hemmerling, *supra* note 6 and Ehrlich, *supra* ch. 1 note 1. *See also* B. Abbin, Gift, Estate and Income Tax Exposures from Recapitalizing Closely Held Companies (unpublished mimeograph, n.d.).

13. The likelihood of an audit depends to some extent on the scrupulousness of the estate planner. It may be that the Internal Revenue Service will not even know of a doubtful valuation until after the statutory period for assessing a tax deficiency has run out. With the filing of a gift tax return, the statute begins to apply to all gifts made during that year including items of supposed zero value, such as common stock in a typical recapitalization, which are not even reported on the return. One planner suggested it was possible to make a small cash gift in the same year as the recapitalization, file a return and pay tax on the cash gift, and thereby start the statute of limitations running on the recapitalization gift without ever mentioning it. The zero valuation for the stock given in the recapitalization must, of course, be made in good faith, because fraud blocks the running of the statute (I.R.C. § 6501(c)). Also, if the undisclosed item is worth more than 25% of the amount of gifts disclosed, the statutory period is extended from three years to six, even if there is no fraud involved (I.R.C. § 6501(e)(2)). Even so, the law seems to offer unwarranted opportunities for trapping the Service with the statute of limitations. *Cf.* Ehrlich, *supra* ch. 1 note 1, at 1681 (suggesting disclosure of recapitalization in sufficient detail on gift tax return will toll statute although no taxable gift is made).

maneuvering), is that the corporation becomes loaded with a heavy preferred dividend requirement and the parent finds himself the recipient of a large amount of ordinary income which has already been taxed at the corporate level. In order for the dividend to have credibility, more cautious practitioners seem to believe it should be cumulative and fixed at a rate somewhat higher than the going rate on similar stock issued by listed corporations, which may get into double figures especially in times of high interest rates. This dividend problem seems to have deterred many recapitalizations in recent years. Other practitioners are, however, willing to try a lower dividend rate or even risk a noncumulative dividend to mitigate its burden. Moreover, everyone concedes that there are certain situations, not unusual, where a parent desires to receive a high current dividend flow from the corporation, or, because of the accumulated earnings tax, has no choice but to accept it. In these situations, the recapitalization fits like a glove and can turn a tax burden into a tax boon. Perhaps for this reason, it has recently been described as "a favorite technique to freeze appreciation in a closely held business."[14] The current status of these recapitalizations was perhaps best summed up by the lawyer who said, "this is as standard as the marital deduction when the proper situation presents itself."

The key, of course, is finding the proper situation. The Salsburys, with a closely held corporation, an expectation of substantial future growth, and a founding father willing to engage in some tax planning, presented a classic, although by no means extraordinary, case. The basic technique can be adapted to a wide variety of other situations, however. We were advised, for example, that forward-looking estate planners encourage their clients to consider a similar arrangement whenever any new venture is being undertaken.[15] At this point, the developer of the new venture can decide exactly how much of the potential he wishes to accrue directly to himself and how much he wishes to bypass him and accrue directly to his prospective heirs. The capital structure can be established accordingly.[16]

14. Moore, *supra* note 10, at 451.

15. *See* Kurzman, *Estate Planning Considerations on the Organization of a Business,* 34 N.Y.U. INST. FED. TAX. 1433, 1434 (1976).

16. This capital structure can include bonds as well as stock to give added tax-planning advantages. *See* Borini, *The Personal Holding Company As An Estate Planning Tool,* 26 U.S.C. TAX INST. 143, 149-50 (1974).

Many interviewees thought that use of dual stock structures in new business ventures was a far more common and more significant area of estate-freezing avoidance than recapitalization of existing corporations. A recent magazine article describing how the privately owned Estée Lauder Company (with estimated sales of $375 million) is being passed on to heirs suggests the potential for use of this strategy on a large scale:

> The Lauder family has come up with a very clever way out. Their highly successful new products—Clinique and Aramis—are actually separate companies. Pick up a bottle and you'll find no mention of Estée Lauder. Substantial holdings in these new companies belong not to the first-generation Lauders but to their sons Leonard and Ronald. [17]

Moreover, there is no reason why this technique need be limited to business ventures. It may be used whenever a wealthy individual wishes to give his spouse or children a slice of his economic future free of tax and yet retain full control. He simply establishes a new corporation with the required two classes of stock and transfers an investment portfolio, real estate, or any other property, to it. The common stock in this new holding company is given to his spouse or children, thereby freeing future growth in value of the underlying property from his estate tax. [18]

This approach can also be used very effectively in situations where there is an existing operating business, as in *Salsbury,* but the existence of outside shareholders or technical problems precludes a direct recapitalization of the operating company. Instead of the operating company being recapitalized, it can be left as is and the client's stock in it transferred to a newly created holding company having the desired stock structure. [19] By using a holding company in this fashion, the client is also free to put in other assets unrelated to the operating business. [20]

17. Minard, *In Privacy They Thrive,* FORBES, Nov. 1, 1976, at 38, 45.

18. Seaman, *Estate Planning for the Real Estate Investor,* 111 TRUSTS & ESTATES 794 (1972), recommends this technique for real estate holdings. The technique, it is said "may offer an individual a good chance of achieving the 'ideal' inter vivos transfer, that is, a transfer which will permit him to retain control over his property so as to limit the possession or enjoyment of the property by others and at the same time will not require inclusion of the full value of the [property] in his taxable estate." Borini *supra* note 16, at 146.

19. Moore, *supra* note 10, at 456.

20. To the extent that passive investments rather than active business operations

The Installment Sale

Another well-known estate-freezing technique is the installment sale. The recent case of John R. Hudspeth provides a good example.[21]

Mr. Hudspeth owned over 1,500 acres of farmland and wanted to transfer a portion of it to his children while retaining use and control for himself.[22] He therefore sold them a portion, having a value of $240,000, in return for nonnegotiable notes and a purchase money mortgage and then leased the land back. The notes and mortgage required each child (there were three sons and two daughters-in-law involved) to pay $7,500 per year to the parents, but the parents in turn were bound to pay $1,500 annual rent to each child and gave each the assurance that annual gifts of $6,000 would be forthcoming, thus providing full coverage of the child's annual obligation. The leases ran for twelve years and were renewable for five more. All of this was worked out in advance and presented to the children, who apparently were adults living apart from the parents, to accept or reject. They all happily accepted since no real risk or burden was involved, and signed the necessary documents. The Internal Revenue Service was rebuffed in its attempt to challenge this transaction as a sham, and has been generally rebuffed whenever it has made a similar challenge.[23]

---

dominate the holding company, it may be classified as a personal holding company for income tax purposes and be required to pay out all current earnings to avoid a stiff penalty tax. *See* I.R.C. §§ 541-47. However, there will be little double tax burden caused by this payout if the bulk of the corporation's income is dividends from stock investments that qualify for the 85% intercorporate dividend deduction (I.R.C. § 243). The remaining 15% of nondeductible dividend income as well as other sources of corporate taxable income can be fully offset in many cases by salaries paid to the owners for managerial services rendered to the corporation, by contributions to fringe benefit programs on behalf of the owner-managers (including such estate planning devices as pension plans and group life insurance programs, *see* text accompanying notes 62-74 *infra*), by payment of interest on bonds held by the corporate owners as part of the original capital structure, and by charitable contributions to organizations favored by the corporate owners. *See* sources cited in note 111 *infra*.

21. Hudspeth v. Commissioner, 509 F.2d 1224 (9th Cir. 1975).

22. Mr. Hudspeth's primary goal was not estate planning but rather the avoidance of Department of Agriculture limits on holdings of irrigated property. Nonetheless, estate planning goals were achieved.

23. *See* Estate of J. W. Kelley, 63 T.C. 321 (1974); Selsor R. Haygood, 42 T.C. 936 (1964). *But see* Minnie E. Deal, 29 T.C. 730 (1958).

The effect of this transaction was to shift immediately from Hudspeth senior to his children all appreciation in the value of property after the date of transfer without any real sacrifice of control or need to pay a gift tax.[24] In addition, to the extent that Hudspeth can develop the property into a superior farm, the ultimate benefit will accrue to his children without tax.[25] The transaction of course did nothing to relieve Mr. Hudspeth's estate of the current value of the farm, since the notes and mortgage received in the transaction were currently equal in value to the land given up. But the transaction was nicely set up so that Mr. Hudspeth could make gifts equal to the annual gift tax exclusion by paying off the notes for his children as they came due (or forgiving them), an opportunity of which he in fact took full advantage.[26] Because we do not know how much the transferred property has increased in value since Mr. Hudspeth made this "sale" in 1966, nor how much more it will increase in the remaining years until his death, the extent of tax saving from this transaction cannot be determined. However, the potential, especially for tax-

24. The parents would be exposed to loss of control after seventeen years because all leasehold rights would then expire and the children would be outright owners of the property. The Hudspeths were willing to accept this risk, possibly because of their age. Other taxpayers have taken the safer course of retaining use for their full lives. Estate of J. W. Kelley, 63 T.C. 321, 322 (1974). In either case, the taxpayer is safe from having the property recaptured into his estate under the retained control provisions of the Internal Revenue Code, §§ 2036-2038, because so long as the transaction is not considered a sham it is a "bona fide sale for an adequate and full consideration," which is exempted from those provisions. Care must be taken to keep the sale bona fide and, in particular, not to tie installment payments directly into income being produced by the property. *See* Greene v. United States, 237 F.2d 848 (7th Cir. 1956); Horvitz, *Retention of Control: The Implication of the Byrum Case,* 32 N.Y.U. INST. FED. TAX 235, 260-61 (1974).

25. If the parent made long-term capital improvements, a portion of the value of such should be deemed a future-interest gift to the children, but most expenditures in developing a farm would seem to have a shorter useful life than the seventeen years of the Hudspeth lease. *Cf.* I.R.C. § 175 (soil and water conservation expenditures generally deductible); I.R.C. § 182 (similar treatment for land clearing expenses).

26. 509 F.2d at 1226. This technique of annual gifts through forgiving installment notes, sometimes known as "piecemeal giving," appears well-known. *See* Richerson, *Are the Tax-Saving Characteristics of Piecemeal Giving in Danger?* 27 TAX LAW. 331 (1974). The writer of the cited article was concerned about the trial court decision in *Hudspeth,* which went against the taxpayer. The eventual result in the court of appeals, discussed in the text, suggests that piecemeal giving is alive and well.

payers who have greater wealth to transfer than Mr. Hudspeth's modest farm, is not difficult to imagine.

The primary advantage of an installment sale such as this occurs when the property sold goes up in value. If it should decline in value, however, the seller has not necessarily lost out on estate planning. It may be possible for him to renegotiate the sale price downward with the buyer (his heir) who has conveniently become a "distressed creditor" due to the decline in value.[27] It is thus possible through an installment sale not only to give away opportunity for appreciation in property while reserving an income from the property but also to take advantage of price declines to reduce the selling parent's estate. Yet no estate or gift tax arises from the sale.

Because of these estate planning advantages, as well as a number of intriguing income tax avoidance possibilities,[28] the installment sale from parent to child (or to a trust for children) has been growing in popularity.[29] Its use need not be limited to situations such as *Hudspeth*, where a parent wants to continue to use property—although

---

27. One such situation was described by an interviewee. A client had owned a substantial block of appreciated corporate stock. Rather than sell it directly and pay a large immediate capital gains tax, he sold it to a trust for his children on an installment sale, thereby shifting future appreciation to the trust while indirectly preserving current value for himself. In this case, unlike *Hudspeth*, the client desired the income from the annual installment payments due from the trust, and the expectation was that the trust would use the income from the stock, plus some sales of it, to make the payments. Shortly after the sale, the market broke and the stock dove in value. At this point the father renegotiated the sale price, dropping it from $2,000,000 to $1,224,000. All the parties expected the stock to go back up in value, but at the time the price could be renegotiated in good faith with his children's trust so that the father could cut $786,000 out of his estate (the reduced value of the installment notes he was holding). This entire transaction, including the price renegotiation, was cleared on audit by the Internal Revenue Service. *See* Rev. Rul. 72-570, 1972-2 C.B. 241.

28. The primary income tax advantage is an ability to defer capital gains tax to the parent, while putting the property in the hands of another person who can make a prompt sale for cash. *Compare* Rushing v. Commissioner, 441 F.2d 593 (5th Cir. 1971) *with* Rev. Rul. 73-157, 1973-1 C.B. 213.

29. One New York interviewee recommended it as the best means of passing on an appreciating art collection to children. Another interviewee, in Atlanta, said that the only limitation on use of the technique was in being able to recognize situations where it could be applied. He then proceeded to reel off a half-dozen instances where he had made effective use of it in recent years. In his view the technique was "almost a natural" in a growing, inflationary economy. Writers in the field have made the same observation. Burch & Hemmerling, *supra* note 6, at 501-04.

that is the most striking use of the technique. Rather it is available and useful whenever estate freezing is desired without incurring current gift tax liability.

The primary disadvantage of an installment sale is that it forces the selling parent to recognize the difference between his basis and the sale price of the asset transferred and pay capital gains tax (albeit pro rata, as installment payments are made or forgiven).[30] This disadvantage, of course, has the offsetting benefit of stepping up the buying child's basis. But that step-up could be achieved, at least for pre-1976 appreciation, without capital gains tax if the property were held until death. One planner, who is enamored of installment sales, said that he resolved this dilemma by providing low current installment obligations with a large balloon payment at the end. This achieves the goal of immediately shifting future growth to the child and puts off the evil day of gain recognition. It also moderates the current payment burden on the child. This balloon payment technique makes it likely that a large portion of the sale price will be unpaid on the parent's death and included as an asset in his estate. To this extent an estate tax will have to be paid on a part of the value of the sold property, but in well-planned cases the capital gains tax attributable to the remaining installment obligations can possibly be nullified, or at least substantially mitigated.[31]

In addition, it appears possible in certain cases to provide, as a part of the original terms of sale, that installment obligations terminate on the death of the selling parent. The effect of this termination is to eliminate all estate taxation of any unpaid obligations, quite an

30. I.R.C. §§ 453(b), 453(d)(1)(B). It has been suggested that recognition of gain can be avoided if installment notes are cancelled rather than given, a rather doubtful verbal distinction. *See* Miller v. Usry, 160 F. Supp. 368 (W.D. La. 1958), *cited in* Warren, *Intra-Family Income Shifting Techniques,* in PLI, ESTATE PLANNING FOR THE LARGE ESTATE 225, 249-50 (1976).

31. If the outstanding installment obligations are bequeathed to the child who is indebted for them, gain recognition may be avoided because possession of debtor obligations and creditor rights in the hands of one person may merge the obligations out of existence. *See* Jack Ammann Photogrammetric Eng'rs, Inc. v. Commissioner, 341 F.2d 466 (5th Cir. 1965), *discussed in* Warren, *supra* note 30, at 250-51. If not, the child as debtor can simply fail to pay himself and thereby never realize gain as creditor. Warren, *supra* note 30, at 251-52. Finally, if neither of these approaches works, the gain when recognized will be treated as "income in respect of a decedent" and the recipient of this income will be entitled to a deduction for the earlier estate tax paid on it. I.R.C. § 691(c).

estate-planning windfall. Yet in the one case where this technique was challenged by the Internal Revenue Service as creating a disguised bequest, the Tax Court rejected the Service position and no estate tax was imposed.[32] Moreover, the Service has indicated, curiously, that it will no longer even seek to impose an estate tax in this situation.[33] Several planners mentioned the potential in this technique, but it does not seem to be used with much frequency, possibly because it seems too good to be true, and the limitations on it have not yet been precisely defined.[34]

Nothing in the Tax Reform Act of 1976 will hamper or impede the development of the installment sale as an estate-freezing technique. Quite the contrary, as in the case of a *Salsbury*-type recapitalization, it may be expected that an indirect effect of the Reform Act will be to generate increased interest in use of installment sales. For one thing, because it involves a "sale" rather than donative transfer, this is another technique that entirely avoids any gift tax (assuming the sale price is fairly set), and it is therefore made more attractive than ever by the new increased gift-tax rates. In addition, the new carryover basis rule for post-1976 appreciation takes much of the sting out of the need to recognize and pay capital gains tax, which was traditionally viewed as the major deterrent to installment sales. When that capital gains tax could be entirely avoided at death, tax planners had an understandable aversion to recommending a quasi-testamentary transaction that necessitated such tax payment. Now, however, the idea of paying the capital gains tax in installments, and,

32. Ruby Louise Cain, 37 T.C. 185 (1961). *See* Ginsburg, *Dividing Income and Capital Appreciation Among Family Members,* 25 N.Y.U. INST. FED. TAX. 645, 665 (1967). The cited article is rich in ideas for income as well as estate tax avoidance and perceptive and prescient in describing many of the techniques discussed herein that have more recently come into flower.

33. *See* 1962-2 C.B. 4 (acquiescence in *Cain*). In one related case, the Tax Court imposed an estate tax on the value of the installments forgiven, on the theory that they were a disguised bequest. That case was, however, a particularly egregious situation, with an exchange of correspondence stating that the transaction should be kept secret to accomplish other tax evasion goals. As such, the court felt compelled to impose a tax and did so more through force of will than logic. Estate of Abraham L. Buckwalter, 46 T.C. 805 (1966). Whether the same result will occur again is doubtful, particularly because, as noted, the Internal Revenue Service has acquiesced in the *Cain* decision.

34. There is a risk that a gift tax could be imposed at the time of original sale unless the payments are set high enough to allow for the reduced value caused by the termination at death. *See* Estate of Sarah A. Bergan, 1 T.C. 543 (1943).

as a by-product, giving the children a step-up in basis equal to the "sale" price, will be viewed in a new light.[35]

Family Partnership

The use of family partnerships to shift income, by bringing a child in as a silent partner, is as old as the income tax, and some of the grosser abuses of the income tax through use of this device have been effectively precluded by court decisions[36] and statutory provisions.[37] One cannot, for example, simply make a minor child a partner in a law firm. However, since 1951, the law has explicitly authorized a shift of a partnership interest to a child, even an infant, where "capital is a material income-producing factor" and the child "owns a capital interest," even if the interest was "derived . . . by gift."[38]

It is thus quite clear that a child can be given a share of ownership in many business ventures. The requirement that capital be a material factor can possibly be satisfied even in the case of a purely service business if the business has goodwill.[39] If the gift is made at an early stage, before the venture has begun to develop its full potential value, the amount of the taxable gift will be quite low, yet a full share of earnings and appreciation will go to the child. This has been described by one writer as "a tax key toward building the family fortune."[40] This expert proposed building up a partnership interest for a client's wife and children with small annual gifts, with no money changing hands; a simple book entry and a deed of gift are all it takes. Moreover, he emphasized that the parent-donor "is free to maintain complete control," as by acting as the managing partner and giving the children limited partnership interests,[41] and that a child's share of

---

35. It should be noted, however, that the Tax Reform Act would probably make it unnecessary for a family farmer such as Mr. Hudspeth to worry about estate tax avoidance. In addition to raising the basic exempt levels, the Act provides a special new valuation procedure for family farms which enables them to be taxed at farming value rather than developmental value. I.R.C. § 2032A.

36. *See* Commissioner v. Culbertson, 337 U.S. 733 (1949); Lucas v. Earl, 281 U.S. 111 (1930).

37. *See* I.R.C. § 704(b)(2), (e).

38. I.R.C. § 704(e).

39. Bateman v. United States, 490 F.2d 549 (9th Cir. 1973).

40. L. GOLDBERG, TAX PLANNING MANUAL 42 (2d ed. 1974).

41. *Id.* at 43. In Bateman v. United States, 490 F.2d 549 (9th Cir. 1973), a parent gave a limited partnership interest to his children in trust, served as trustee of the trust, and acted as general partner of the partnership, all without adversely affecting

annual profits need not be paid out but can be retained for business growth to further augment the child's capital share. These benefits can be even further enhanced with more sophisticated structuring of partnership interests.[42]

Despite these many estate-planning advantages obtainable from partnership manipulations, there appears to be relatively little ex-

---

the shift of partnership interest to his children under the income tax law. The estate tax rules regarding trust powers are a bit different from the income tax rules but most easily managed by having the spouse of the donor-parent serve as trustee. *Compare* I.R.C. § 671 *with* I.R.C. §§ 2036, 2038.

42. Among the most impressive uses of family partnerships described to us were situations that made effective use of borrowed funds to leverage the potential for shifting value to children. Suppose that a partnership is created for a new business venture. The father, who is a real estate entrepreneur, becomes the general and managing partner and makes a modest contribution to capital. His children become limited partners, making a capital contribution equal to or even larger than their father's. The substantial funds needed for the project are borrowed from banks or other independent lenders. To the extent that the transaction succeeds, the banks or other outside lenders are paid off and the overriding gains accrue to the children in proportion to their capital contributions. But if the transaction fails, the parent as general partner is left holding the major share of the liability. Thus the child has been presented with a risk-free opportunity for substantial gain, free of transfer tax. New I.R.C. §§ 465, 704 (d) would preclude use of this leveraging technique in many situations but would have no effect on real estate transactions, where primary use seems to be made of it.

Other planners have aided the shift of value to children by layering partnership interests to separate future growth from present value, thereby creating an advantage such as Dr. Salsbury gained from his stock recapitalization. This is done by providing that a parent has a primary, but limited, claim on income and the children have a secondary, but open-ended, claim to long-term appreciation. Such an arrangement has the added advantage of enabling the parent to claim credit for the initial tax losses so often produced in a partnership venture. Care must be taken whenever unusual allocations of a partnership interest are created, because of income tax provisions which upset unusual allocations to any family member in a family partnership when such allocations are disproportionate to his capital contribution (I.R.C. § 704(e)), or when such allocations do not have "substantial economic effect" (new I.R.C. § 704(b)(2)). However, so long as the allocations represent a fair arm's-length bargain (such as trading off a small primary income interest for a larger but more speculative longer term interest) and have real economic significance and estate planning value, and the parent is paid a reasonable salary for his management services, it would appear that the adverse impact of these provisions can be avoided. *See* S. REP. NO. 94-938, 94th Cong., 2d Sess. 98-101 (1976); Kuney v. United States, 524 F.2d 795 (9th Cir. 1975); Rev. Rul. 68-139, 1968-1 C.B. 311; Lee, *The Partnership "Special Allocation": When Will It Be Upheld: Orrisch Analyzed*, 43 J. TAX. 138 (1975). In any event, these special income tax provisions have no analogue in the estate and gift tax law, so even if these provisions are invoked, their implications for transfer taxation are problematic.

ploitation of them by estate planners. The legal rules in this area are much less settled than the rules regarding corporate interests, and most planners seem to prefer the additional certainty of corporate arrangements even at the loss of some flexibility. The partnership potential remains in stand-by status, however, ready to be developed into a major planning technique rivaling corporate manipulations if there is any significant foreclosure of corporate avoidance mechanisms. Moreover, the Tax Reform Act, while making some changes in partnership tax rules, did little to close off its potential as an estate tax avoidance tool.[43] Until these techniques are developed further, however, use of the family partnership is more appropriately considered as part of the more general category of intrafamily diversions, to which we now turn.

The Intrafamily Diversion

The technical legal planning that underlies much of the estate freezing discussed above is not always necessary. Any approach whereby a wealthy individual can divert a wealth-generating opportunity to his prospective heirs can fairly be classified as estate freezing, even though the parties engaging in it may not be conscious of the substantial estate-planning implications of their actions. There is no doubt, as mentioned earlier, that a wide variety of the typical layman's estate planning of this nature is a basic part of the regular activity of many wealthy individuals. Especially if one is an active businessman or investor, opportunities for bringing one's prospective heirs into a profitable activity occur with regularity.

The extensive audit of Richard Nixon's tax returns by the Joint Committee on Internal Revenue Taxation provides a good example of how a child can profit, without gift tax, from parental advice.[44] Patricia Nixon (Tricia) received a substantial sum on reaching her twenty-first birthday in 1967 from a trust fund established on her behalf by Elmer Bobst, a family friend. She loaned $20,000 of those proceeds to her father in return for his demand note bearing interest at 6 percent per annum. The father and daughter entered into a claimed oral understanding that this sum would be invested in a Flor-

43. *See* note 42 *supra.*

44. Jt. Comm. on Int. Rev. Tax, Examination of President Nixon's Tax Returns for 1969 through 1972, S. Rep. No. 93-768, 93d Cong., 2d Sess. 147-55 (1974).

ida land development venture known as Cape Florida Development Co., Inc., in which Mr. Nixon was also making an investment. Tricia was to have no management or control over the investment. The joint investment was made in 1967 for $38,000. In 1972 the property was sold for $150,000 and $65,000 was paid to Tricia as her share of the proceeds.[45]

This transaction was scrutinized in a tax audit that was as expert and exacting as any ever conducted and, after much discussion and legal analysis, the Joint Committee took pains to say that if the transaction had been properly established with a binding obligation to pay Tricia a fixed share of the profits at the outset, it would be fully recognized for tax purposes.[46] However, the Committee also found that the claimed oral agreement was not sufficiently established by the evidence to be creditable. Mr. Nixon was therefore subject to income tax on the full profit from the deal, and the Committee suggested that the payment of Tricia's profits to her should be treated as a gift from Mr. Nixon. For our purposes, the critical point is that there was nothing fundamentally challengeable about the deal. If it had been cleanly carried out it would easily have succeeded in enriching the young woman by $45,000 in a single investment transaction through the exploitation of her father's knowledge and contacts and without any gift tax to him.

This transaction is a typical example of what all our interviewees acknowledged was a common and ordinary practice. The extent to which the younger generation in a wealthy family is enriched in this fashion is impossible to estimate, but it is surely an important factor in assuring that the children of wealthy parents themselves become wealthy.

Despite the obvious implications of such diversions for maintaining the level of family wealth from generation to generation, it would be foolhardy to suggest that every such diversion is or should be within the reach of the estate or gift tax. No sensible person would suggest that a tax could be imposed on the giving of parental advice. Frequently, however, these diversions involve more than mere advice, as the parent provides his child with a valuable opportunity,

45. The money was not in fact paid to Tricia but rather was paid to C.G. Rebozo and Rebozo signed a three year 8% note to her. *Id.* at 150.
46. *Id.* at 154.

created by the parent, whose economic worth is a direct reflection of the parent's activities. These additional factors are what turns many family partnerships into effective transfer tax avoidance devices, and they should raise doubts when they appear in other contexts as well.

A striking example of a situation where a parent effectively shifted a portion of the value of his own business activities, as distinguished from merely sharing investment advice, is provided by the case of *Robert P. Crowley,* an income tax case which has impressive estate planning implications.[47] Mr. Crowley controlled a savings and loan association. The operation of this business generated various collateral sources of income—appraisal fees, insurance fees, and abstract and title policy commissions. In 1952, he set up a partnership (later incorporated), Crowley Co., to handle this collateral work. The partnership was wholly owned by Crowley's four children in equal shares, all of which were held in trust by Mrs. Crowley for the benefit of the minor children (ages nineteen, sixteen, fourteen, and ten). The partnership's initial working capital came from $2,000 contributions from each child, funded out of the child's small personal savings account. The oldest son, still in college, had received some training in appraisal work from his father, and he handled such work for the partnership with his father's assistance. The appraisal fees were divided between the association and the partnership. The son also acquired a license as an insurance agent and he handled the insurance needs of the savings and loan association, serving as subagent of several general insurance agents. Abstract and title fees were handled similarly. The partnership (later incorporated) generated $57,000 in income from these sources for the children in three years, without any income tax (or, presumably, gift tax) being paid by the father.

This case should not be taken to mean that any such diversion will be successful. In the *Crowley* case itself we learn of one instance that went too far. Mr. Crowley, before setting up his children's partnership, had engaged in a small personal loan business of his own. He tried to divert this business to the children by advancing them money at 2½ percent to be loaned to his former customers at 6 percent. The court taxed the income from these loans directly to Mr. Crowley.[48]

47. 34 T.C. 333 (1960), *acq.,* 1961-2 C.B. 4. *See* Ginsburg, *supra* note 32, at 654-55.

48. 34 T.C. at 347. As a matter of simple logic it would seem that this loan in-

The theory of the *Crowley* court was that the various fees for appraisal and insurance services were at least colorably earned by the children, while the loan income was strictly payment for use of the parent's capital and not, as the court puts it, "from the performance of services, however meager" by the children.[49] The Internal Revenue Service acquiesced in this decision without qualification. A prudent tax planner should not be lulled by this acquiescence into total reliance on the Tax Court's "however meager" standard, but the possibilities for tax-free diversions suggested by this case need not be ignored either. If a diversion to minor children of a business wholly controlled by a parent can escape tax, how difficult can it be to divert more subtle opportunities to adult children?[50]

The author of one recent article strongly recommends such diversion strategies for wealthy parents "to prevent buildup of equity in their corporations and to permit the effective transfer of values to the next generation without transfer tax being incurred."[51] Many of our interviewees were more explicit. They described situations where a parent directed business to a new corporation owned by children, helped it out with inventory, and supported it with his experience in a myriad of ways. In some instances the parent actually served as an officer or employee of the new company and took principal responsibility for running it for a modest salary.[52]

The common factor in all these transactions is the transfer to a child of valuable parental talents and services, which are seemingly

---

come should also have been considered a gift to the Crowley children, as it was earned and vested in them, but the gift tax was not an issue in the case, and we may fairly wonder whether any gift tax was in fact collected.

49. *Id.*

50. One planner, familiar with the activities of real estate speculators, described how a person with whom he was acquainted diverts his talents to the benefit of his children. This planner explained that the speculator looks at a hundred deals for every one in which he finally invests. This screening process is a sophisticated full-time activity. By enabling his children to participate in the deal finally selected, the parent is in effect giving them immensely valuable services.

There are some obvious nontax limitations on these diversions of business opportunities imposed by the law of corporate opportunity, the fiduciary obligations of a partner, and the securities laws, but these are hardly comprehensive.

51. Miller, *Certain Aspects of Estate Planning for the Business Owner,* 33 N.Y.U. INST. FED. TAX. 81, 98-99 (1975).

52. Where the parent participates to the extent of actually running the business, the situation is essentially similar to a family partnership described above except that the children are 100% owners rather than only fractional owners.

not subject to the gift tax. Because this strategy also has income tax avoidance implications, the income tax law has some provisions that could be used to attack more obvious abuses, as where a parent runs a business owned by his children for a grossly inadequate salary.[53] However, these provisions would not cover many of the situations described above,[54] and in any event, what little law there is on the subject suggests that, even where these provisions do apply, their effect does not carry over to the estate and gift tax. That is to say, even if income of a child is reallocated to his parent for income tax purposes to reflect the parent's real contribution to a business, it does not necessarily follow that this income, which still legally belongs to the child, will be treated as having been obtained by gift from the parent.[55] Our interviewees agreed that there were broad opportunities for the rendition of services from parent to child with no real risk of estate or gift-tax exposure.[56]

Another form of intrafamily benefit that seems to have escaped the coverage of transfer taxes despite its obvious economic value is loans from parent to child. All of the planners with whom we spoke said that clients frequently loaned funds to enable their children to undertake business or investment opportunities. To the extent that such loans are made at prevailing rates of interest and arm's-length regularities are observed, there seems to be no risk of transfer taxation even if the child's credit would not have enabled him to obtain a similar loan from a stranger. Moreover, many instances were reported in which the loans were made interest-free or at low rates. The Internal Revenue Service takes the position that the amount of interest forgone in this fashion is a taxable gift,[57] but has had trouble con-

53. I.R.C. §§ 704(e)(2), 1375(c).

54. For example, these provisions do not, by their terms, have any application to a Subchapter S corporation situation in which the parent is only an employee and not a shareholder. *Compare* I.R.C. § 1375(c) *with* I.R.C. § 704(e)(2). Nor do they seem to have any application to cases such as that of the real estate speculator, described in note 50 *supra,* where the parental services are indirect and not rendered to a business as such.

55. In Hogle v. Commissioner, 132 F.2d 66 (10th Cir. 1942), income produced by a parent's management of a margin trading account for his children was taxed to the parent, but in a later case the court refused to charge the parent with having made a taxable gift to his children. Commissioner v. Hogle, 165 F.2d 352 (10th Cir. 1947).

56. *But cf.* I.R.C. § 482; Ginsburg, *supra* note 32, at 656-57.

57. Rev. Rul. 73-61, 1973-1 C.B. 408.

vincing the courts of this.[58] Moreover, in most cases, unless the loan is very large, the amount of interest forgone will be less than the annual gift-tax exclusion and will not even come to the attention of the Service.

A variation on this loan arrangement, which is also very popular, is for parents to guarantee repayment of loans obtained by children from banks or other third parties. It seems clear that such a gift of credit is not subject to transfer taxation.

Another nontaxable benefit that parents frequently provide for children is the assumption of risk of loss so that children can undertake opportunities they might otherwise fear. This assumption of downside risk, with children having all or a large part of the opportunity for gain in a transaction, is an important feature of many of the techniques already discussed. It occurs, for example, in the *Salsbury*-type recapitalization, where if the business declines in value the parent's preferred stock bears the full burden of the loss; all the children can lose is the chance of gain. Similarly, in most installment sales the selling parent's only security for payment of the installment notes is a lien on the property involved. If it goes down in value rather than up, the parent must simply foreclose and take it back (or, as mentioned earlier, if he believes the decline to be temporary, he can take advantage of the situation to renegotiate the sale price downward).[59] The assumption of risk aspects of certain partnership arrangements were discussed above. Sometimes the assumption of risk is not rolled into a more complex arrangement but is simply a direct and unfettered assurance from parent to child. An assurance of this nature was part of the Nixon Cape Florida deal discussed earlier, in that Mr. Nixon guaranteed to Tricia that, at a minimum, he would return her basic $20,000 investment to her.[60] Yet the Joint Committee nowhere suggested that this assumption of risk generated any tax problem.[61]

---

58. *See* Lester Crown, 67 T.C.—No. 88 (1977); Johnson v. United States, 254 F. Supp. 73 (N.D. Tex. 1966). *But cf.* Mason v. United States, 513 F.2d 25, 30 n.15 (7th Cir. 1975) (charitable deduction allowed for interest forgone).

59. *See* note 27 *supra*.

60. *See* Jt. Comm. on Int. Rev. Tax, *supra* note 44, at 147.

61. If it ever becomes necessary for a parent to make good on a guarantee against loss, a gift will occur at the time that the parent covers the child's loss unless the child obligates himself to repay. *See* H.R. Rep. No. 94-658, 94th Cong., 1st Sess. (1975). For this reason, the *Salsbury*-type situation, where the parental burden

It is thus possible, with as much facility after 1976 as before, for a parent to devote great effort to locating investment opportunities for his children, to provide the capital to exploit these opportunities, to supply expert personal services that will make the opportunities a success, and to assure that if, after all this, the deal fails, he will pick up the loss—all without any transfer-tax liability.

Creating Tax-Exempt Wealth

Estate freezing, by diverting future income and gain directly into the hands of one's prospective heirs, is a planning strategy of major importance to wealthy business owners, entrepreneurs, investors, and others whose activities naturally generate capital growth. This group accounts for a large segment, if not a majority, of all wealthy individuals. But what about another rich group, the high-salaried executive or other person whose "wealth" is primarily a high level of current income? Such a person can, of course, make annual gifts of portions of his income and thereby gradually build up the wealth of his family, but that is a slow process if one is simply taking advantage of the annual exclusions and requires gift tax payments if the process is accelerated. Fortunately for these persons, other avoidance techniques are provided by law, tailored to their needs. The answer for such persons is to take advantage of legal opportunities for the creation of tax-exempt wealth.

Life Insurance

The most significant item in this category is life insurance. This was frequently described by our interviewees as the single most important weapon in the planner's arsenal and it remains unaffected by the Tax Reform Act. One use of life insurance by an individual with a high income flow is to create an immediate substantial estate on behalf of his prospective heirs with the insurance, to fund payment of the premiums on that life insurance with annual gifts to the beneficiaries, and yet to pay little if any transfer tax because of gift tax exclusions. For example, annual gifts of $6,000 exempt under the gift tax exclusion will buy more than $300,000 of ordinary life insur-

---

simply inheres in the arrangement rather than manifesting itself as a separate promise, is a superior avoidance strategy.

ance for a forty-five-year-old man and even greater amounts of term insurance.[62] However, such use of life insurance, while yielding valuable benefits, is simply a means of making effective use of the gift tax exclusion.

The more impressive transfer-tax avoidance technique is to provide life insurance for prospective heirs without transferring funds in a manner cognizable under the gift tax law. This opportunity is available to corporate executives who are commonly the beneficiaries of large amounts of employer-funded group term insurance.[63] It is not unusual, we were told, for executives to have $500,000 or even $1 million of such insurance. The incidents of ownership in this insurance can be assigned to prospective heirs or to a trust on their behalf and thereby be excluded from the executive's estate. However, since the executive is not paying premiums on the insurance, he never reports any gifts on account of it, no matter how high these annual premiums may be.

This scheme seems vulnerable under existing law on the theory that the employer payments are an indirect gift made on behalf of the executive to the beneficiaries of the insurance. Since 1964, the value to the executive of such premium payments has been recognized under the income tax law as a fringe benefit and taxed to him to the extent it exceeds $50,000 of death value.[64] However, there is no similar explicit provision in the gift tax, and planners took the position that the gift tax law is sufficiently vague on the matter to justify ignoring all employer premium payments under that law. They noted that they have not been challenged on this point by the Internal Revenue Service. Subsequent to our interviews, the Service did issue a revenue ruling asserting that a taxable gift is made by an employee when his employer pays premiums on life insurance vested in his beneficiaries.[65] However, whatever success the Service may have in enforcing this ruling, it is clear as a matter of current practice that many corporate executives have insurance estates of many hundreds of thousands of dollars on which no estate or gift tax has been paid. Moreover, since this insurance arrangement can be used for ordinary

62. *See* Teachers Insurance and Annuity Association, Life Insurance Guide (Pamphlet 1974).

63. *See* Rev. Rul. 72-307, 1972-1 C.B. 307.

64. I.R.C. § 79.

65. Rev. Rul. 76-490, 1976-50 I.R.B. 28.

insurance as well as group term, since there are no legal limits on the amount of insurance provided, and since closely held family corporations, where the top executives are also the owners and shareholders, are as eligible to provide this insurance as public corporations, the possibilities for exploiting this avoidance technique even further—if the Service does not make its new ruling stick—are staggering.[66]

The Company Annuity

Another major source of tax-exempt wealth for corporate executives is amounts payable to their heirs under qualified employer-funded pension and profit-sharing plans. Such amounts, even though they are an important source of enrichment passing indirectly from the employee to his heirs as a result of his work and effort, are specifically exempted from estate taxation by section 2039(c) of the Internal Revenue Code. Moreover, under section 2517 no gift tax is payable on the source of funding for these death benefits—employer contributions during the executive's lifetime. Dr. Salsbury, whose stock recapitalization was discussed earlier, managed to avoid taxes on an additional $61,600 because of section 2039(c).[67] Other taxpayers undoubtedly have gained even greater benefit.[68]

It is difficult to find any continuing justification for this gap in the estate tax base. It is surely not necessary to protect impoverished spouses, since the regular estate tax exemptions and deductions assure that this provision will not even be relevant until an estate reaches $425,000. Nonetheless, though for years reformers have urged Congress to repeal section 2039(c),[69] the major response in the Tax Reform Act was to expand it. The provision now covers individual retirement plans as well as the employer-sponsored variety.[70]

---

66. For example, a recent report suggested that the owner of a giant, privately held supermarket chain had several hundred million dollars in company-provided life insurance. *See* Minard, *supra* note 17, at 45.

67. Estate of Joseph E. Salsbury, 34 T.C.M. (CCH) 1441, 1454-55 (1975), discussed at text accompanying notes 3-12 *supra*.

68. Miller, *supra* note 51, at 113-16.

69. *See* ALI, FEDERAL ESTATE AND GIFT TAXATION, RECOMMENDATIONS ADOPTED BY THE ALI AND REPORTERS' STUDIES 15-16 (1969).

70. *See* new I.R.C. § 2039(e). The section was curtailed somewhat to preclude coverage of lump-sum distributions from plans.

The Survivorship Benefit Plan

The amount of benefits that can be provided pursuant to section 2039(c) is limited by the fact that the benefits must be payable under a qualified plan and the rules governing such plans call for the inclusion of lower-level employees without discrimination. However, it appears that other survivorship payment arrangements, outside the context of a qualified plan, are "experiencing a surge of popularity."[71] In these arrangements an agreement is entered into between the corporation and one or more top executives, whereby, in consideration of the executive continuing to work for the corporation until his death, it will pay a substantial sum to his surviving spouse or other beneficiary. In several litigated cases the value of such benefits has been held not to be an asset includible in the executive's estate and taxable to him on his death.[72] These cases all arise in the context of closely held corporations where it is clear that the payments have been worked out as a means of passing corporate wealth to the surviving beneficiary, and while the estate tax avoidance implications of the arrangement are thus obvious, they do not seem to have impressed the courts.

Internal Revenue Service officials with whom we spoke acknowledged the seriousness of this problem and indicated that plans with death benefits as high as $200,000 were not unusual. But the only defense seemingly open to the Service to combat this practice, if the present cases are not overturned, is to tax the value of the survivorship benefit as an indirect gift from the executive to his future beneficiaries at the time that the agreement is entered into. One court has implied that it would support application of the gift tax in this manner.[73] However, an article by a leading practitioner discussing the technique expresses surprise at the suggestion that the gift tax might be so applied, clearly indicating that it is not current practice to report it as such on gift tax returns.[74] The Internal Revenue Service, therefore, has a difficult problem on its hands in even discovering such arrangements in time to apply the gift tax. Moreover, even if a

71. Miller, *supra* note 51, at 121.

72. *See* Kramer v. United States, 406 F.2d 1363 (Ct. Cl. 1969); Hinze v. United States, 29 A.F.T.R.2d 72-1553 (C.D. Calif. 1972); Harris v. United States, 29 A.F.T.R.2d 72-1558 (C.D. Calif. 1972).

73. *See* Porter v. Commissioner, 442 F.2d 915 (1st Cir. 1971).

74. *See* Miller, *supra* note 51, at 123.

transaction is discovered promptly, the value of the gift would have to be discounted to take account of the fact that it will not actually be paid for some time. In addition, the value would have to be further reduced to take account of the fact that ultimate payment is dependent on the contingency that the executive continue his employment until his death. Many plans, it was reported to us, further complicate the valuation problem by making the death benefit a fixed percentage of the employee's salary at death, an amount obviously unknown and unknowable at the inception of the plans.

All of this suggests that the Internal Revenue Service will at best collect a small partial tax on these survivorship benefit plans if and when they are tracked down.

Disposing of Accumulated Wealth

The preceding discussion concerns itself with the means by which a wealthy person can put a ceiling on his estate through various techniques that move future accumulations to his prospective heirs free of tax. But what about wealth accumulated before such strategies are put into effect? This is more difficult to deal with, and planners warned that the secret to much of effective estate planning is to start early enough. A dollar in hand is worse than two in the bush from an estate-planning perspective. Nonetheless, there are measures that can be taken to minimize the amount of transfer tax even on amounts previously accumulated and, indeed, means whereby that tax may be wholly avoided.

The Gift Tax Exclusion

The most important technique for avoiding high taxation of extant wealth has traditionally been the making of lifetime gifts. Many tax planners suggested that it is seldom realized how much wealth can be moved this way with little tax. They stressed that the annual exclusion of $6,000 per beneficiary for a married taxpayer is an especially important aspect of a gift-giving plan and often all that is necessary to make an entire estate plan effective for a person of modest wealth.

Consider, for example, the case of a married individual in his fifties, with an accumulated estate of $1 million, and a classic American family consisting of two married children and four grandchildren. If this person included the spouses of his children in a gift-giving program, there would be eight potential beneficiaries of gifts, which, at $6,000 per beneficiary per year, would enable him to give away $480,000 of his million dollars in only ten years, free of any gift tax at all. By doing this, plus making an additional large gift of $60,000 to take advantage of the basic gift exemption available under old law, and then bequeathing half his remaining estate to his widow to take advantage of the marital deduction, the hypothetical millionaire could have reduced his estate tax under pre-1976 law to only $41,700. It was thus possible, without any elaborate planning, to reduce the total transfer tax bill for a person with $1 million, a normal family, and a normal life span, to only 4 percent of that $1 million, probably less than the sales tax the person would have had to pay had he spent all his money before his death.[75]

How does the Tax Reform Act, with its higher gift tax rates, affect this situation? Not at all. Indeed, the tax bill for our typical millionaire will be even lighter under the new law. The Tax Reform Act leaves the crucial annual exclusion untouched. Thus the $480,000 of tax-free exclusion gifts can be made just as before. Moreover, because the basic amount exempt from estate or gift taxes (on top of the annual exclusions) has now been raised so dramatically, almost nothing of the remaining $520,000 will be subject to tax. If our friend simply bequeathed that remaining sum to his wife, taking maximum advantage of the marital deduction, his estate tax bill would be a mere $31,700, down to only 3 percent from the stiff 4 percent he faced under old law.[76]

And the above figures make no mention of the built-in estate-freezing benefits, which naturally flow from a gift-giving program. The assets transferred could well be something that is appreciating and, if so, this future appreciation is shifted from parent to child without tax. Finally, it should not be assumed that this gift-giving

75. If the widow gave nothing away during her remaining life, she too would have had, under pre-1976 law, an additional tax of $41,700 to pay, but she could have reduced this to little or nothing by continuing the gift-giving program.

76. Here, too, the surviving widow would face a matching estate tax bill of $31,700, unless, as is likely, she opts to continue the gift-giving program. Also, it should be noted that the above calculation assumes that our hypothetical friend survived for three years after making his last gift. If not, the new § 2035 would recapture one-half (but not all!) the annual exclusion gifts made within that three year period, causing a modest increase in his tax bill.

program entails total loss of control over the property by the donor. As noted earlier, these gifts can, for example, take the form of a minority interest in a corporation over which the parent maintains continuing voting control.[77]

Spending Money on Heirs

If direct gift-giving is not sufficient, there are endless indirect ways in which a parent can spend sizable sums on behalf of his children without incurring transfer taxes and thereby, in effect, shift accumulated wealth to them. In the area of business and investment, perhaps the most effective technique is for a parent to bear the primary risk of loss in a transaction, which is structured so that any big gain accrues to the children. Such arrangements were discussed above.[78] They are "heads I win, tails the government loses" deals for estate planning purposes, since losses reduce a parent's wealth, which is presumably in a higher bracket and nearer to the date when tax will fall due, and gains enhance a child's wealth, which is presumably in a lower bracket and far from the day of taxation.

One tax planner related a story of an extreme arrangement that vividly illustrates how indirect expenditures can be used with devastating effectiveness as a wealth transfer device. A parent owned a large tract of potential oil land. He believed that producing wells could be brought in; but that was not certain and in any event would require large exploratory expenditures to determine just where on the tract the oil could be located. He divided this tract into a checkerboard and deeded all but a narrow strip in each square to his children. There was little tax to pay because the oil potential was so uncertain and the expected exploration cost so great. The parent then proceeded to spend the necessary sums searching for oil on his little strips while his children stood by as observers. Finally when he located a producing area, the parent was enriched to the extent that his little strip had increased in value. This may or may not have been enough to offset the exploratory costs involved. But the major value of the discovery accrued to the children who could focus their drilling efforts in a low-risk, high-yield way.

This story has the air of Texas exaggeration about it, but the point

77. *See* text accompanying note 18 *supra*.
78. *See* text accompanying notes 59-61 *supra*.

that it makes can be adapted to a wide variety of investment situations. Many tax planners might caution against going into tax avoidance on such grand scale, because the lesson has been learned that overreaching in avoidance brings trouble. But there seems little question that if the same approach is used in a series of separated drilling ventures (dividing the property between parent and child and having the parent take the lead in undertaking exploratory risk), it will not be vulnerable under present law.

The Private Annuity

Unless a parent has vast wealth—in the multimillion dollar category—a gift-giving program combined with expenditures and risk-bearing on behalf of a child will be more than adequate to transfer tax-free as much wealth as he wishes to transfer, if, and this is a big if, the parent lives long enough after embarking upon his estate plan. Unexpected death will wreak havoc with this sort of estate planning. It may be suspected that nature is in this way an important ally of the Internal Revenue Service; if everyone knew exactly when he was going to die, perfect estate planning would be easier, and much less tax would be collected. Estate planners can, however, sometimes fool Mother Nature, at least to the extent of guarding against some of the adverse planning implications of early death.

One estate-planning antidote for mortality, already discussed, is the use of an intrafamily installment sale with prearranged cancellation of payment obligations on death of the seller.[79] Another, more commonly known, technique, which is actually a variation on the same theme, is the private annuity—that is, an annuity arrangement not involving an insurance company or similar institution.[80] In a typical transaction, a parent transfers property to his children in return for a promise from the children to pay him a periodic fixed income.[81] If the transaction is "ideal," the annuitant transfers virtually all his property in payment for the annuity and dies the day after transferring the property. He has no estate tax to pay because

79. *See* text accompanying notes 32-34 *supra.*

80. Nonprivate annuities are of no value here because (1) the property ultimately winds up in the hands of a stranger, the insurance company, and (2) an immediate capital gain tax must be paid on any untaxed appreciation in the property transferred.

81. The annuitant must forgo any security interest or continuing control over the

he owns no property at his death. There is no gift tax to pay and no transfer in contemplation of death because, assuming that a fair annuity amount was set, the property was sold for an annuity—a transfer for full consideration—rather than given away. No income tax on appreciation in the property need be paid because no annuity payments were actually received.[82] Yet, despite the absolute freedom from tax, all the decedent's property is now in the hands of the next generation. Morbid as it may seem, several planners described, with some pride, private annuity transactions that had succeeded in this fashion because the annuitant had cooperated by dying promptly.

On the other hand, if the annuitant lives to his full life expectancy or most of it, the estate planning advantages of the transaction quickly fade. The periodic payments to him will total the full value of the property with 6 percent interest. (Unless the payments were set at this arm's-length level, the transaction will be viewed as a disguised gift.) The property will thus circle back and the annuitant will have paid an ordinary income tax on the interest component of the payments as well as a capital gains tax on any appreciation that had accrued on the property at the time of original transfer. He will thereby lose the opportunity to exploit the capital gains tax avoidance opportunities available on property held until death. And if the annuitant is so vigorous as to live longer than the actuarial tables predict, he will win on his annuity but lose on his estate planning to the extent that more will come back than he originally laid out and that his prospective heirs will enrich him, rather than vice versa.[83]

---

transferred property to avoid having it recaptured for his estate. *Compare* Estate of Lloyd G. Bell, 60 T.C. 469 (1973) *with* Fehrs Fin. Co. v. Commissioner, 487 F.2d 184 (8th Cir. 1973), *cert. denied,* 416 U.S. 938 (1974). *See also* Mark Bixby, 58 T.C. 757 (1972), *acq.* 1975 I.R.B. 12, at 6; Simon M. Lazarus, 58 T.C. 854 (1972), *aff'd,* 513 F.2d 824 (9th Cir. 1975).

82. A capital gains tax on appreciation accrued to the time of transfer is payable but only pro rata, as annuity payments are received. Rev. Rul. 69-74, 1969-1 C.B. 43. *See* Warren, *Intra-Family Income Shifting Techniques,* in PLI, ESTATE PLANNING FOR THE LARGE ESTATE 225, 254 (1976).

83. One possible estate-planning advantage to an annuitant who lives as long as or longer than his life expectancy is that appreciation in the transferred property subsequent to the creation of the annuity will not be taxed to his estate. But this estate-freezing benefit could be achieved more easily with a simple installment sale. A classic example of a long-lived annuitant who nonetheless succeeded in estate planning is the case of Pierre S. du Pont, who arranged a private annuity in 1924. This is surely one of the earliest examples on record of this tax avoidance plan.

For all these reasons, the private annuity is frequently viewed by planners as an estate planning gamble, which, because of the by-product income tax effects, is not even a good actuarial bet. The usual comment about it is that it is "the most discussed, least used" technique in estate planning. But this critical judgment holds only if one is playing it straight; if some way can be found to beat the actuarial tables, the assessment of the value of the gamble changes dramatically. The principal means by which the tables are beaten has already been alluded to above. Private annuities are established by persons who, for reasons of health or otherwise, have cause to doubt whether the figures in the tables apply to them. One planner described the case of "a widow in poor health" where "it was a good bet she wouldn't last too long." She transferred a valuable farm to her children in return for an annuity and died within one year. Another planner told of using the private annuity several times for clients who were "sickly." The Internal Revenue Service has the power under present law to override the actuarial tables in situations where persons are involved whose life expectancy is in very serious doubt,[84] thus enabling it to challenge these transactions in gross situations. However, none of the planners who admitted to playing the odds in this manner indicated that the Service had raised any question even in the cases where the technique had been very effective. The general view both among estate planners and within the Internal Revenue Service seems to be that only a fully manifested terminal illness at the time of creating the annuity will provide a basis for challenge.[85]

Property worth $13.5 million was transferred to a du Pont family holding company in return for a promise to pay Pierre S. and his wife an annuity of $900,000 per annum until the death of the survivor. Pierre died in 1954 at age eighty-four, having collected a total of $27 million on his original investment. However, the property transferred had increased in value to $127 million by 1927 and was worth well in excess of a half billion dollars by the time of Pierre's death. *See* Paulina du Pont Dean, 19 T.C.M. (CCH) 281, 284 (1960); Mary A.B. du Pont Laird, 38 B.T.A. 926, 934-37 (1938); M. DUKE, THE DU PONTS, PORTRAIT OF A DYNASTY 308 (1976). The sudden increase in value of the transferred property, from $13.5 million in 1924 to $127 million in 1927, suggests that the tax-planning benefits here were helped out with a little fudging on initial valuation, a subject we take up at length momentarily. *See* text accompanying notes 86-113 *infra*.

84. *See* Lion v. Commissioner, 438 F.2d 56 (4th Cir.), *cert. denied,* 404 U.S. 870 (1971); Dunigan v. United States, 434 F.2d 892 (5th Cir. 1970).

85. Another way of beating the tables is to invest the transferred property and earn a good enough rate of return to more than cover the 6 percent rate on which

The Valuation Discount: The Strange Case of Disappearing Value

All noncash gifts or transfers at death subject to estate and gift taxation must of course be valued, and an extraordinarily productive technique for reducing taxes on these transfers is to exploit valuation uncertainties. Aggressive tax lawyers have developed a package of valuation stratagems which cut deeply into the estate and gift tax base. They have succeeded to a shocking extent in winning judicial approval of these techniques and Internal Revenue Service acquiescence in them. As a consequence it appears possible, with a bit of advance planning, to have transfer taxes apply to as little as one-third of the real value of property transferred by gift or bequest. The remaining value simply disappears for transfer tax purposes, thanks to valuation discounts.

The principal vehicle for obtaining these discounts is a closely held corporation. The valuation of stock in such a corporation is a problem that has long plagued analysts and generated much confusion and uncertainty. A common view is that there is no one answer that is clearly correct and that a process of horse-trading goes on. The taxpayer sometimes gets the best of the bargain, the government sometimes gets the best, and, in general, results even out over the long run despite occasional aberrational cases. However, our discussions with practitioners and a detailed examination of the trends in reported cases reveal that this conventional view is wrong. Taxpayers are running circles around the Internal Revenue Service in the valuation process.

---

the annuity must be calculated for tax purposes. This is very difficult to do in ordinary situations, since income taxes must be paid on earnings from the property, but there is some discussion in estate-planning literature about using foreign trusts to facilitate high earnings. *See* Kanter, *New Decisions Delineate Tests for Foreign Situs Trust-Private Annuity Transactions,* 38 J. TAX. 82 (1973); Kanter, *Recent Tax Court Decisions Shed Further Light on Private Annuity Transactions,* 42 J. TAX. 66 (1975). If the transferred property is put in a trust in a tax haven, such as the Bahamas, its earnings are not subject to current income tax, making possible the necessary high rate of after-tax return. However, this opportunity is closed off by the Tax Reform Act (new I.R.C. §§ 668, 679) and, in any event, the technique seemed too fishy even without such reform to appeal to most planners. It may be worth noting that the principal proponent of this arrangement has recently been indicted for related matters. *See* N.Y. Times, Mar. 5, 1976, at 12, cols. 1-2. It is possible, however, that other approaches to beating the tables will be developed with a broader appeal. *See* ch. 3 text accompanying notes 25-26 *infra.*

A standard procedure has developed in closely held corporation stock valuation cases, which can best be analyzed as a two stage process, although courts and most analysts frequently blur the stages. In the first stage, a base value for the corporation is determined by reference to the book value of underlying assets, the current and potential earning power of the company, the company's dividend record, the values of stock in similar publicly traded companies, and other criteria. In virtually all cases, both the taxpayer and the government call in expert appraisers as witnesses, and the appraisers (frequently more than one on each side) present their competing analyses of base value. This is a highly subjective process and is difficult to second-guess. Many planners suggest that the Internal Revenue Service loses in this process, but a close reading of cases suggests that many came out fairly enough.

If this first stage were all there was to the valuation process, particular cases might well be questioned, but it would be difficult to be very critical of the overall outcome. The real problem comes in the next stage.

This second stage is the application of a series of special factors which cause the fair market value of the corporation's stock to depart from the base value of the corporation itself. The major factors that have been recognized are:

1. *Blockage.* When the block of stock being valued is very large, its prompt sale may depress the market.[86]

2. *Unmarketability.* Stock of a closely held corporation, which is not normally traded and therefore not well known to prospective buyers, may accordingly suffer in sale value.[87]

3. *Minority interest.* If the block of stock being valued does not have voting control, buyers may be discouraged, especially when they would be buying into a family situation.[88]

4. *Costs of flotation and sale.* If there is no established market, it may be necessary to have an underwriting to sell the stock, with attendant costs.[89]

---

86. *See* Treas. Reg. § 20.2031-2(e) (1974).
87. *See, e.g.,* Estate of Ernest E. Kirkpatrick, 34 T.C.M. (CCH) 1490 (1975).
88. *See, e.g.,* Estate of Maurice G. Heckscher, 63 T.C. 485 (1975).
89. *See, e.g.,* Inga Bardahl, 24 T.C.M. (CCH) 841 (1965).

5. *Restrictions on disposition.* Frequently in family-owned corporations there are limitations or restrictions on the disposition of stock, which inhibit its sale and discourage buyers.[90]

6. *Capital gains and other tax liabilities.* In certain situations, there may be a substantial unrealized gain on the assets of the corporation or other latent tax liability, which may depress its value in the eyes of a buyer who is purchasing with a view to liquidate.[91]

It is obvious that several of these factors overlap, and no case has been so foolish as to allow for all of them in a single situation. However, many cases have allowed for one or more factors that seem to be duplicative.[92] Worst of all, the courts and even the expert appraisers representing the government allow for these factors in cases where the allowance makes absolutely no sense from the viewpoint of intelligent estate and gift tax enforcement. For example, blockage may be a genuine problem for someone who is actually forced to unload a major block of stock in a distress sale, but what relevance does it have to someone who has no such need?[93] The lack of voting control suffered by a minority interest may be a substantial problem for a stranger to a family corporation, but it hardly has the same meaning to the partial owner of a corporation whose spouse owns enough additional stock to provide control.[94] Problems of marketability, costs of flotation, and restrictions on disposition may bother someone who plans to sell stock, but for the owner of a chunk of a family business he intends to keep, these matters may be beside the point. Indeed, in many cases, so-called valuation discount factors may actually enhance the value of stock to the owner, as in the case of a restriction on disposition which is part of reciprocal restrictions

90. *See* Hartwig, *Valuing an Interest in a Closely-Held Business for the Purpose of Buy/Sell Agreements and for Death Tax Purposes,* 26 U.S.C. TAX INST. 215, 266-67 (1974).

91. *See, e.g.,* Mary A.B. du Pont Laird, 38 B.T.A. 926 (1938).

92. *See, e.g.,* Estate of Maurice G. Heckscher, 63 T.C. 485 (1975); Estate of Harry G. Stoddard, 34 T.C.M. (CCH) 888 (1975); Paulina du Pont Dean, 19 T.C.M. (CCH) 281 (1960).

93. *See, e.g.,* Whittemore v. Fitzpatrick, 127 F. Supp. 710 (D. Conn. 1954); Mary A.B. du Pont Laird, 38 B.T.A. 926 (1938).

94. *See, e.g.,* Sundquist v. United States, 34 A.F.T.R.2d 74-6337 (E. D. Wash. 1974), *decree entered,* 35 A.F.T.R.2d 1606 (1975); Obermer v. United States, 238 F. Supp. 29 (D. Hawaii 1964).

on other shareholders.[95] Yet, in case after case, the courts apply these factors, seemingly oblivious to the special family circumstances in which the valuation is being made. The ultimate result is an estate planner's dream.

An examination of the facts in a few typical cases will give a sense of the extent to which these valuation discounts have opened the door to wholesale erosion of the estate tax base. A classic is the case of *Whittemore v. Fitzpatrick*.[96] Mr. Whittemore owned all 820 outstanding shares of the J. H. Whittemore Co., a holding company. He gave 600 of these shares to a single trust for his three sons, and the court was called upon to value these shares for gift tax purposes. The company apparently held most of the property of Mr. Whittemore, worth a total of some $2.65 million. He was, by these gifts, effectively transferring almost three-fourths of his wealth to his children.

The children did not pay a gift tax on three-fourths of the value, however. First, the court noted that one of the assets of the company was a major block of stock in a traded corporation (18,366 shares of Peter Paul, Inc.), and allowed an 11 percent discount from the open market price of that stock to allow for blockage. There was not the slightest suggestion that anyone planned to liquidate this block of stock, but the approach of the court was to discuss everything in terms of what would happen if things were sold immediately. This blockage discount reduced the value of the holding company by $92,000. Continuing in the same vein, the court then noted that a prospective purchaser of the holding company might be discouraged by many of its illiquid assets (which apparently included the family art collection) and by other factors and would pay substantially less than the aggregate value of the assets held by it. This justified a 50 percent discount from net asset value (already reduced for the blockage on Peter Paul, Inc.) to take account of marketability problems. Finally, the court noted that there were three individual sons and concluded that it was valuing three separate 200 share blocks, each of which was a minority interest, despite the fact that the stock was all held by the same two trustees, and this justified a 16 percent increment to the discount.

95. *See* Feld, *The Implications of Minority Interest and Stock Restrictions in Valuing Closely-Held Shares,* 122 U. Pa. L. Rev. 934 (1974).

96. 127 F. Supp. 710 (D. Conn. 1954).

The end result was a gift tax value of $1,057 per share, even though the value of the underlying assets transferred, without the three discounts, was $3,233 per share. Mr. Whittemore's gift tax (assuming no other gifts) was thereby reduced by approximately $400,000. Moreover, if, on his death, his remaining 220 shares were valued in the same way, he stood to save another $158,000 in estate tax. The aggregate gift and estate tax bill on this $2.65 million fortune under pre-1976 law (and assuming no marital deduction) would have been only $187,000, which is an effective rate of 7 percent. The same transactions after the Tax Reform Act would bear a slightly higher tax, $247,000, which is an effective rate of only 9 percent.

Whittemore is an astounding case, but it is by no means singular. For example, in *Paulina du Pont Dean*,[97] the Tax Court had to value gifts of minority blocks in Nemours Corporation given by Ms. Dean to trusts for her children. Nemours was an investment holding company wholly owned by Ms. Dean and her husband. Its only significant assets were 13,000 to 14,000 acres of timber and farmland, $2 million of notes receivable from Mr. and Ms. Dean, and a block of stock in Delaware Realty and Investment Company. Delaware Realty, in turn, was a du Pont family-owned holding company whose major assets were blocks of stock in du Pont Company and in Christiana Securities Co. The latter was the premier du Pont family-owned holding company, with large blocks of stock in du Pont Company and General Motors, having an aggregate market value in excess of $2 billion.

The court began its valuation by determining the asset value of Christiana from market values of its underlying traded securities. It then allowed a 21 percent discount from this asset value for Christiana stock and attributed that discounted value to the Christiana stock held by Delaware Realty. This provided an asset value for Delaware Realty, on which the court then allowed a further 14 percent discount, to arrive at a value for the Delaware Realty stock held by Nemours. As for the land held by Nemours, since this was primarily used by the Deans for horse breeding and generated no income (actually it produced large annual losses), it was given a negligible value of $94.33.

97. 19 T.C.M. (CCH) 281 (1960).

Having determined the asset value of Nemours in this fashion, the court then allowed a third 20 percent discount from that asset value for the gifted Nemours stock to take account of its minority interest nature, its blockage problems, and the fact that the poor Nemours stock was "thrice removed" from the real source of its income. In justifying this final discount, the court also noted that Nemours had losses on its horse breeding operations and was burdened with personal loans to the Deans. The end result was a value of $640 per share. If the stock had been valued without the successive discounts piled on discounts and a modest $100 per acre value for the land, the value would have been $1,120 per share. This is a somewhat smaller percentage saving than that obtained by Mr. Whittemore, but since Nemours was a $40 million corporation the potential tax saving was much larger—in the tens of millions.

The court in *Dean* did resist a further argument, advanced by the taxpayer's expert appraiser, that the value should have been further reduced to allow for problems of blockage and a latent capital gains tax on the du Pont and General Motors stock held by Christiana. The court reasoned, in a show of good sense that was later overwhelmed by its discount doublecounting, that these stocks had been held for many years and there was no plan to sell them.

This should be contrasted with *Obermer v. United States*.[98] In that case, a husband and wife each owned 50 percent of a holding company that owned, in the court's words, only "readily marketable securities—namely blue-chip stocks sold every day on the New York Stock Exchange, and held in blocks not so large as to call for any discount for shares sold in large blocks."[99] Nonetheless, when the husband died and bequeathed his 50 percent interest to his wife, the court allowed a discount of 33.33 percent from asset value, largely because a noncontrolling interest was involved and because the underlying shareholdings had a large latent capital gains tax, both of which would be very troublesome to a buyer of the bequeathed stock. Yet neither of these matters was necessarily any problem to the individuals involved. Since his spouse owned the other 50 percent of the corporation, Mr. Obermer did not suffer the usual burdens of a minority owner. And with regard to the latent capital gain, the fact

98. 238 F. Supp. 29 (D. Hawaii 1964).
99. *Id.* at 32.

that the property was passing through an estate created a unique opportunity to avoid that tax burden. As heir to her husband's interest, Ms. Obermer took that interest with a stepped-up basis and could, through some complex tax maneuvering, use that new basis to avoid the capital gains tax liability on half the property in the corporation.[100] If she had inherited the underlying property directly, no one would have suggested that its value be reduced on account of the capital gains tax that need not be paid. For some reason the existence of the corporation led the court astray.

The justification usually advanced for these deep discounts is that stock in publicly traded closed-end investment companies, which the corporations in these cases resemble, frequently sells at a substantial discount from asset value. However, these traded companies are ones in which an individual purchaser who acquires a small minority interest will have to deal with strangers and will have no influence over management and investment decisions. The self-created family holding companies in the cases above, which are undoubtedly run with the narrow interests of the family members carefully in mind and over which the family members as a group exercise control, do not pose the same issues. Moreover, many of the factors that result in discounts on closed-end investment company stock, such as a latent capital gains tax on asset holdings, may not be a problem for a family holding company, as noted above. In spite of these distinctions, the discounts allowed by courts are excessive even by the standards established in the closed-end investment company market.

Estate of Maurice G. Heckscher[101] provides a good example. Mr. Heckscher died owning a small (2.3 percent) minority interest in a family investment company, Anahma Realty, established by his father. The asset value of the company's investments, consisting of marketable securities and large holdings of Florida land, was $193.42 per share ($21 million in total). This valuation allowed for a discount of 10 percent on the land to take account of real estate commissions and other selling expenses that would be incurred if it were sold (although there was no suggestion of imminent sale).

100. *See* Milefsky, *How to Use a Personal Holding Company as an Effective Estate, Financial Planning Tool*, 42 J. TAX. 202 (1975).

101. 63 T.C. 485 (1975). The information discussed in the text is based on an examination of the Tax Court record in this case as well as the reported opinion.

After determining this asset value, the Internal Revenue Service appraiser consulted a *Wall Street Journal* listing of closed-end investment company prices as of the appropriate date and discovered that these prices ranged from a discount of 31.6 percent to a premium of 74.9 percent on asset value. The average for all was a 10.6 percent discount, and the average for only the discounted companies was minus 20.2 percent. Yet the Service appraiser allowed a 30 percent discount, almost the lowest of the low, on top of the real estate discount already allowed. He added to this a further reduction of $23 per share to allow for the costs of floating an underwriting of Mr. Heckscher's shares. All of this brought the value per share down from an asset value of almost $200 to $112 per share.

The court considered this analysis and compared it to the expert appraisal submitted on behalf of Mr. Heckscher's estate which, through reliance on an elaborate set of questionable assumptions, had produced a valuation of $60 per share. The court rejected this alternative approach in favor of that of the Service expert but then chopped the valuation by another $12 per share on the ground that the discount allowed seemed too small. The final valuation, $100 per share, was half of asset value.[102]

The Internal Revenue Service at one time fought against the allowance of these discounts.[103] But the trend in the cases, which are appearing in growing numbers, has become so clear that discounts are allowed as a matter of course and the only argument seems to be over size.[104] The Service seems almost complaisant on the matter.

102. *See also* Estate of Alvin Thalheimer, 33 T.C.M. (CCH) 877 (1974), *aff'd*, 532 F.2d 751 (4th Cir.), *cert. denied*, 97 S. Ct. 317 (1976), *on remand*, 36 T.C.M. (CCH), T.C. Mem. 1977-3, 1977–49 (1977) (discounts of 34% to 37% in situation similar to *Heckscher*).

103. *See, e.g.*, South Carolina Nat'l Bank v. McLeod, 256 F. Supp. 913 (D.S.C. 1966).

104. There has been a small explosion in reported minority discount cases, which have increased from 18 in the 1950–59 decade and 21 in the 1960–69 decade ,to 24 in the 1970-75 period, 15 of which have occurred in the past two years. Moreover, the discounts allowed in these cases have been steadily increasing. *See* Dant, *Courts Increasing Amount of Discount for a Minority Interest in a Business*, 43 J. TAX. 104 (1975). (This article includes a list of cases that is incomplete and understates the discounts allowed in some cases. For example, *Paulina du Pont Dean* is indicated as a 20% discount case, ignoring the cumulative discounts allowed by the court which aggregated more than 40%, as our discussion at text accompanying note 97 *supra* shows.) (Note continued on page 52.)

Our interviewees confirmed that the Internal Revenue Service regularly opens negotiations with discounts of 20–25 percent in minority interest situations and goes to 40 percent in settlements. The Service's own valuation experts propose discounts of 50 percent for minority interests,[105] and in at least one recent case both the Tax Court and the court of appeals found a higher valuation ($37 per share) than the Service had thought possible to claim ($25 per share).[106] One writer has even argued that discounts are too low and

---

Moreover, even cases which appear at first glance to be taking a stricter line on valuation turn out on further examination to be quite generous to the taxpayer. For instance, Feld, *supra* note 95, discusses Estate of Pearl Gibbons Reynolds, 55 T.C. 172 (1970), as an example of good reasoning by the courts on valuation. In this case the court was called upon to value voting trust certificates (the equivalent of stock without the vote) in a family-controlled life insurance company. The sale of these certificates was restricted in that they had to be offered to other family members for a formula price ($283–$316 in the key years) before being sold on the open market. The market price, based on modestly active over-the-counter trading of the stock with vote, was eight to nine times higher than the formula prices ($2,540–$2,637 in the same years). The court wisely rejected the argument that the formula price should control, taking the position that the recipients of the certificates intended to hold them and that "retention value" rather than sale value was the key. But the court then went on to allow some reduction of unstated amount, to take account of the sale restriction. It also allowed a discount for the lack of vote on the units, even though it conceded that the voting trust arrangement (which shifted the vote to trustees who held voting control and acted on behalf of the certificate holders) "was probably a benefit and certainly would not be considered a detriment," *id.* at 192, to the persons involved, because a buyer of the units might be concerned about it. In so doing, the court slid away from its retention value approach. The final value arrived at ($1,500–$1,700 in the years mentioned), while substantially higher than the formula price sought by the taxpayer, involved a discount from market value essentially similar to those in the other cases discussed above. Similarly, in Silverman v. Commissioner, 538 F.2d 927 (2d Cir. 1976), the court fully supported the Service and rejected a minority discount claim in arriving at a $37 per share value for closely held stock, but the market value based on a public offering of the stock within a year was $70 per share. And in Driver v. United States, 76-2 U.S. Tax. Cas. ¶ 13,155 (W.D. Wis. 1976), the court rejected unrealistic claims for minority discount and discount for sale restrictions on stock but then gave heavy weight to marketability discounts, arriving at a $55 per share value for stock having an open market value of $110 according to Service experts.

105. *See, e.g.*, Estate of Ernest Kirkpatrick, 34 T.C.M. (CCH) 1490 (1975). *Cf* INTERNAL REVENUE SERVICE, IRM 4350, AUDIT TECHNIQUE HANDBOOK FOR ESTATE TAX EXAMINERS ¶ 6(11)6 at 48-49, *reprinted in* 2 IRM (CCH) 7626; MANHATTAN DISTRICT, I.R.S., REPORT ON AUDIT TECHNIQUES, VALUATION OF BUSINESS INTERESTS FOR ESTATE TAX ATTORNEYS 27-29 (both sources suggest minority discounts should be questioned but seem to assume that they are commonly allowed).

106. Silverman v. Commissioner, 538 F.2d 927 (2d Cir. 1976).

should go as high as 90 percent.[107] The Tax Reform Act of 1976 essentially ignores this valuation discount problem. The only provision that even bears on the matter is a new procedure requiring the Internal Revenue Service to disclose and support its valuation assertions when assessing a deficiency, as if the Service were not already having enough trouble.[108]

The Service does seem to be trying, as a modest way of offsetting the lost tax base caused by minority discounts, to argue for an offsetting majority or control premium in cases where that is applicable. The pickings have been slim, however. The major case in which a control premium was allowed is *Estate of Joseph E. Salsbury,* the recapitalization case discussed at length earlier.[109] Here the Tax Court added a 38.1 percent premium to the value of Dr. Salsbury's retained preferred stock, in recognition of the voting control this stock had over the entire corporation. Unfortunately, this percentage was not applied, as the Service sought, to the value of the entire corporation or to the value of the common stock, both of which were worth many millions of dollars. Instead, the court added 38.1 percent to the value of the preferred stock itself, which was worth only $372,152. Given this approach, the control premium is unlikely to have much effect.

The ultimate effect of these discount developments was foreseen by the Tax Court many years ago in one of the earliest cases discussing the issue. There the court denied the discount, with a prescient observation:

If the arguments of petitioner were to prevail, any cohesive family owning securities having a market value readily ascertainable from trading on the open public market could organize a family holding corporation, transfer to such corporation the securities which it owns, and then deal with the stock of the family corporation on the basis that it has by reason of petitioner's arguments a market value of only approximately half of the market value of the securities owned by such a corporation, thus cutting in two gift taxes and estate taxes which would otherwise be payable on the transfer of the securities themselves.[110]

107. Moroney, *Most Courts Overvalue Closely Held Stocks,* 51 Taxes 144 (1973).

108. *See* new I.R.C. § 7517.

109. *See* text accompanying notes 3-11 *supra.*

110. Richardson v. Commissioner, 2 T.C.M. (CCH) 1039, 1047 (1943), *aff'd,* 151 F.2d 102 (2d Cir. 1945), *cert. denied,* 326 U.S. 796 (1946).

This case seems to have been forgotten, and planners today are doing exactly as the court anticipated, for the message of the valuation discount cases is too striking to be ignored.[111] Several interviewees admitted to putting property in a corporation and a series of minority interests in trusts for children and claiming full discounts. Moreover, by the time the parent dies, if all goes according to plan, he will be left holding only a remaining minority interest, thus gaining a discount for his estate and avoiding even the risk of a control premium. To the extent that the parent in such a situation imposes restrictions on the gifted stock to keep some restraints on his prospective heirs, he not only accomplishes a personal goal but also enhances the possibility of obtaining reduced valuation. Moreover, he can use the corporation as a vehicle for transferring illiquid family property, such as the art collection in *Whittemore* and the hobby farm in *Dean,* and add still another argument for reduced valuation, even though these items are ones he would presumably wish to transfer to his children in any event.

The transfer of property to a personal holding company does generate some disadvantages under the income tax, primarily the forcing of substantial ordinary income, in the form of dividends to the corporate owner, and some exposure to double taxation. Without going into a detailed analysis of these problems, we only note that the several taxpayers whose cases have just been discussed, as well as many of our interviewees, seemed to feel that these income tax problems were tolerable. This is certainly true if most of the holding company's income is derived from dividends on corporate stock, 85 percent of which is deductible by the holding company.[112] Several other techniques are available to counteract other income tax problems and, indeed, even turn them into estate-planning benefits.[113]

While the use of closely held corporations in the manner described offers the most impressive possibility for obtaining valuation discounts, there is some room for similar manipulations with regard to

111. *See* Borini, *supra* note 16; Milefsky, *How to Use a Personal Holding Company as an Effective Estate, Financial Planning Tool,* 4 J. TAX. 202 (1975); Neuwahl, *Incorporation of a Portfolio Consisting of Marketable Securities—A Useful Tax-Planning Technique,* 28 U. MIAMI L. REV. 395 (1974); Ehrlich, *supra* ch. 1 note 1, at 1678-79.

112. *See* I.R.C. § 243.

113. Some of these techniques are mentioned in note 20 *supra. See also* the articles cited in note 111 *supra.*

property held in a noncorporate form, particularly real estate. Several cases have awarded the equivalent of a minority discount to holders of partial interests in real estate, such as undivided one-half interests. The theory is that such owners are subject to restrictions on use and control that undercut the value of their holdings, even where the other half interest is held within the immediate family. However, these discounts have been smaller—on the order of 15–25 percent— than the massive discounts obtained in the corporate cases.[114]

While the Tax Reform Act does not speak to this problem, it does add a major new string to the taxpayer's valuation discount bow in cases involving family farms or real estate used in other closely held businesses. Such can now be valued at farming (or other business) value rather than full market or developmental value, if certain conditions are met.[115]

The Conservation Easement

Another valuation-reducing tactic for real estate that is growing in popularity is the creation of conservation restrictions or easements that do not interfere with the desired use by the owner but that nonetheless cut seriously into sale value. The primary example of this is the creation of open-space easements that are donated to charitable conservation organizations.[116] These easements do not give the donee organizations any rights to use the property but merely the right to prevent designated uses by the owner or anyone else. Many types of restrictions qualify as deductible open-space easements, including limits on future construction or on the removal of trees.[117] If the easement is created during life, the donor gains the benefit of a current charitable income tax deduction plus the estate and gift tax benefit of reduced property value. (A further benefit of this reduced value is that it lessens local property taxes.) If a client does not want to bind himself to restrictions during his life, it is possible to postpone the creation of an easement until death by providing for it in his will.

114. *See* Drybrough v. United States, 208 F. Supp. 279 (W.D. Ky. 1962); Estate of Horace K. Fawcett, 64 T.C. 889 (1975); Estate of Louis D. Whitehead, 33 T.C.M. (CCH) 253 (1974).

115. *See* new I.R.C. § 2032A.

116. *See* Rev. Rul. 73-339, 1973-2 C.B. 68; Rev. Rul. 74-583, 1974-2 C.B. 80; Browne & Van Dorn, *Charitable Gifts of Partial Interests in Real Property for Conservation Purposes*, 29 TAX LAW. 69 (1975).

117. Treas. Reg. §§ 20.2055-2(e)(2)(i) (1974); 1.170A-7(b)(1)(ii) (1975).

This achieves the advantage of reduced estate tax values, although it does forgo income tax benefits.

The Tax Reform Act gives new impetus to the creation of these easements by providing the first explicit statutory authorization for them.[118] The use (and abuse) of this technique accordingly is expected to grow.

One interviewee described an example of such an easement, the case of a fishing lodge surrounded by a large, rustic area which the owner wanted to preserve in its primitive condition. The owner donated to a charitable organization an easement barring any construction or development of the rustic area, thus preserving it as a natural sanctuary. This drastically reduced the taxable value of the property without altering the owner's use. A major sacrifice is involved here in that the owner has forgone important potential rights, and the tactic is therefore of no value to most landowners. But for a very wealthy owner, who is confident that he and his heirs will desire continued personal or recreational use of an estate indefinitely, such a contribution may be viewed as a tax windfall.

The Trust for the Very Rich

The package of techniques covered thus far should, if properly exploited, be sufficient to reduce the estate and gift tax to a nuisance level for all but the very richest fraction of a percent of the population, that is, the super rich, whose wealth is counted in tens of millions of dollars. This is an extremely small group. According to the best available data, only 194,073 families, representing 0.3 percent of all families, had more than $1 million of net wealth in 1972[119] and only 2,400 persons, 0.002 percent of the adult population, had more than $10 million.[120] The smallness of this group increases rather than

118. *See* new I.R.C. §§ 170(f)(3)(B)-(C), 2055(e)(2), 2522(c)(2). This statutory authorization is scheduled to lapse in 1981, but past practice suggests that extension is likely.

119. *Hearings, supra* Intro. note 1, at 1311, 1318 (statement of Prof. James D. Smith).

120. Telephone conversation with Prof. James D. Smith, Pennsylvania State University, July 2, 1976. In talking to estate planners we regularly asked specific questions about estates in excess of $10 million. No one even blinked. Some cautioned that they had few clients in that category, while others seemed to have many, but no one treated the question as hypothetical. On this basis, it is probably fair to guess that we spoke to planners of a hundred $10 million estates in our modest series

diminishes its importance for purposes of this report. Vast wealth is concentrated in these few hands,[121] and they are the focus of the concentration break-up policy that has been suggested to support estate and gift taxation. Some might argue that this group is the only one that warrants serious concern for estate and gift tax purposes. Even if transfer taxes fail to hit hard at smaller fortunes, as the preceding discussion suggests to be the case, they are nonetheless worthwhile if they succeed in cutting down the accumulated fortunes of the super rich. Unfortunately, however, just as massive wealth generates other benefits, it creates special estate-planning opportunities, which blunt most of the force of transfer taxation.

The most important of these special techniques has traditionally been the generation-skipping trust. As is well known, use of such trusts has been largely limited to the very rich, probably because other estate planning techniques, not involving long-term trusts, have been adequate for the less wealthy.[122] For the most wealthy, however, such trusts have posed fewer disadvantages, since large sums of money would have probably been held in some form of investment fund in any event and since the intervening generation could be given the equivalent of absolute ownership of trust assets through powers of appointment and trust powers.[123] These trusts have offered incredible transfer tax avoidance benefits. For an intervening generation now the beneficiary of a generation-skipping trust, estate planning is no problem, because the trust is already the best possible built-in estate plan. Moreover, although in most states the tax benefits of a generation-skipping trust are limited effectively to two generations by

---

of interviews, which would be a major fraction of the total. Prof. Smith suggests that our interviewees may have confused gross wealth with net worth, but even so the numbers accounted for in our study are large enough to suggest that we covered a significant segment of the very wealthy. Eventually, however, it may be necessary to increase the estimates of numbers of top wealth-holders to reflect the implications of this book. The major source of data for current estimates is estate tax returns which, according to our findings, grossly understate actual wealth.

121. Professor Smith's best estimate, for 1972, is that the $10 million plus group held $69 billion of net worth, 2% of the national total. Telephone conversation, *supra* note 120. While this is not bad for a group constituting only .002% of the adult population, it may nonetheless be substantially understated, as noted in the preceding footnote.

122. *See* C. SHOUP, *supra* ch. 1 note 8, at 39-44.

123. *See Hearings, supra* Intro. note 1, at 1333-36 (statement of Prof. A. James Casner); S. KESS & B. WESTLIN, CCH ESTATE PLANNING GUIDE 179 (1976).

the rule against perpetuities, it appears possible to create (in at least Idaho and Wisconsin) a perpetual trust, permanently eliminating future transfer taxes.[124]

The perpetual generation-skipping trust may have been the ultimate estate-planning scheme for those who had the foresight to establish one. It is, however, too late for less foresightful mortals to avail themselves of this grand stratagem or even of a more modest, one or two generation-skipping arrangement. The Tax Reform Act, in its most aggressive gesture against estate tax avoidance, has provided a special new tax on all generation-skipping trusts, which is designed to tax these arrangements more or less as if the intervening generation actually owned the property held in trust. This new tax is by no means a death blow to all generation-skipping trusts since it exempts all existing arrangement for all time (including, presumably, perpetual versions), exempts any generation-skipping trust provided for in an existing will so long as the testator dies before 1982,[125] and, in addition, permanently exempts the sum of $250,000 per child of a decedent.[126]

Moreover, it remains to be seen how effective the new provisions will be in taxing property every generation even when that property can no longer make use of a generation-skipping trust. For example, estate planners are already formulating an alternative that avoids the new generation-skipping tax.[127] Under the alternative, the bulk of a fortune is given directly to a second or third succeeding generation (grandchildren or great-grandchildren of the donor) in a trust controlled by the first succeeding generation (children of the donor) but in which the first generation has no beneficial interest. The financial needs of the first succeeding generation can be met with a generous outright gift of principal which they are free to consume. The trust avoids any tax on the included property for a generation or two and yet is exempt from the generation-skipping tax because only a single generation has beneficial interests in it.[128] Indeed, the committee re-

124. *See* 1 A. CASNER, ESTATE PLANNING 675 (3d ed. 1961). Our research indicates that the laws in these states remain today as described by Professor Casner, and we have heard of at least one such trust having been created in Wisconsin.

125. Tax Reform Act of 1976, Pub. L. 94-455, § 2006(c), 90 Stat. 1888.

126. New I.R.C. §§ 2613(a)(4), (b)(6).

127. *See* Covey, *Generation-Skipping Transfers,* in PLI, THE TAX REFORM ACT of 1976 305 (1976); Metrick, *Generation Skipping Transfers,* in *id.* at 391, 423.

128. *See* new I.R.C. §§ 2611(b), 2613(c)-(d).

port on the 1976 Act makes clear that one or more children of a donor can be trustees of a trust and can have discretionary powers to allocate income among their children (grandchildren of the donor) and to invade principal for their children, all without invoking the new tax.[129]

Whatever the outcome of these attempts to maneuver around the new generation-skipping tax, it is clear that the provision will have an effect in increasing the exposure of at least some wealthy persons to estate and gift taxation. This is not a new circumstance, however. Even before 1976, there were very wealthy persons who were not protected from tax by the umbrella of a generation-skipping trust. This group included, for example, the nouveau riche who had not had a chance to come under a generation-skipping umbrella, and the generations in an established wealthy family on whom the remainder interest from a skipping trust had been deposited. These persons have not been devoid of tax avoidance routes in the past and they will not suffer from such lack in the future.

For such persons, our interviewees agreed, a major alternative to high transfer tax payments was, as one earthy planner put it, "to do the charitable bit." This can, and frequently does, take the form of bequests to existing charitable organizations. Often it results in the creation of a foundation. Both these routes to charitable giving result in a permanent loss of funds to the family, although that loss can be somewhat mitigated in the case of a foundation by giving the family a continuing role in controlling it. There is, however, a third route to charity which offers just as much in the way of tax saving and gives a lot more to one's heirs. In fact it gives the heirs most of the benefits of complete ownership.

The device that produces these marvelous results is known as a charitable front-end annuity trust or a charitable lead annuity trust. In such a trust, property is held to pay a fixed sum annually to charity for a period of time (this is the front-end or lead period), and at the end of that time full ownership of the property and all income there-from reverts to noncharitable beneficiaries, such as the heirs of the trust's creator. When property is placed in such a trust, whether by gift or bequest, the creator of the trust receives a charitable deduction for the actuarial value of the front-end annuity interest, determined

129. *See* H.R. REP. No. 94-1380, 94th Cong., 2d Sess. 49 (1976).

under Internal Revenue Service tables.[130] For example, if $10 million is put in trust to pay $600,000 per year to charity for twenty-four years, the charitable deduction is $7,530,240. This deduction, roughly equal to three-fourths the estate tax value of the property put in trust, would effectively eliminate three-fourths or more of the estate tax liability on the trust property.

At first blush this tax result seems reasonable enough, since the individual has given up $14,400,000 (24 × $600,000) of income over the twenty-four-year period to obtain a $7,530,240 deduction, and the difference is the 6 percent discount factor built into the tables. However, such simple reasoning fails to take account of income tax effects. For persons of such great wealth, a current $600,000 return would produce a net benefit of only $180,000 after taking account of income taxes. That is to say, if the individual had earned $600,000 per year and contributed it to charity, the net sacrifice to him would have been only $180,000 per year in the sense of after-tax income forgone. Thus, the more accurate way of appraising this front-end trust is to say that the individual has given up $4,320,000, spread out over twenty-four years (24 × $180,000), the present value of which is $2,259,072. For this he has gotten an immediate estate tax deduction that, assuming an estate tax rate of 70 percent (which is the new maximum rate set by the Tax Reform Act), produces an immediate in-pocket benefit from reduced estate taxes of $5,271,168—more than double the amount sacrificed. Viewed in this way, the front-end trust is quite a desirable technique for those who are in the high brackets where this beneficial rate trade-off occurs. Once the discount factor is canceled out, for each $100 the Treasury forgives $70 in return for the taxpayer sacrificing $30 to charity.

The benefit from creating a front-end trust is enhanced if one can earn more than the 6 percent rate built into the tables on property placed in trust. If, for example, the funds are invested in bonds paying 8 percent interest, $10 million will produce an annual annuity of $800,000 which, with the 6 percent discount, is the equivalent of placing $13,333,333 in trust, and the deduction is increased accordingly. If an $800,000 annuity runs for twenty-four years, the char-

---

130. I.R.C. §§ 2055(e)(2)(B), 2522(c)(2)(B); Treas. Reg. § 20.2031-10 (1970); Treas. Reg. § 25.2512-9 (1970).

itable deduction computed under the tables is $10,040,320—slightly more than the full amount of the $10 million given to the trust. In other words, it is entirely possible to claim a charitable deduction for the full amount of property placed in trust even though the charity is being given only a temporary interest in the property and the full amount of it is eventually going free and clear to one's heirs.

The front-end trust is especially attractive when one realizes that the thing given up, current income for a limited period of time, is a relatively unimportant aspect of property for the very wealthy. Persons in the wealth categories we are now discussing have more current income than they can expend. Beyond a certain point, the real value of greater wealth is power, control, and security. These things are hardly sacrificed at all in a front-end trust. Ultimate total ownership and control after the annuity period provides ultimate security. And during the intervening annuity period, the remainder beneficiaries can serve as trustees and thereby control the property. They will, of course, be restricted by the legal rules defining fiduciary responsibility and certain of the tax rules governing private foundations and generation-skipping trusts.[131] These tax rules impose significant restrictions on the extent to which the trust property can be diverted to the personal benefit of the family during the trust period.[132] However, nothing in these rules should prevent most reasonable uses of the property, including a flexible investment policy.

The analysis necessary to understand the advantages of a front-end trust is not simple, and it has not yet been grasped by many estate planners.[133] It is, however, sufficiently beneficial that it is being

---

131. *See* I.R.C. § 4947(a)(2) (private foundations); § 2613(d) (generation-skipping trusts). The most significant restraint is probably that imposed by new I.R.S. § 2613(d), which requires that the trustee-beneficiaries forgo any current power to allocate income or corpus from the trust, including a power to allocate among charitable beneficiaries, in order to avoid taxation as a generation-skipping trust. However, this problem can be avoided either by fixing the charitable beneficiaries in the trust instrument or by giving any discretion in this regard to an independent trustee who likely will be responsive to the family's wishes.

132. I.R.C. § 4941.

133. A significant number of planners are still lamenting the passing of that time, before 1970, when they could set up a front-end trust paying "all income" to charity, claim a large deduction, and then invest the trust property in assets producing a low rate of return (but high capital appreciation), so that the charity got less than the amount of the deduction and the heirs got a windfall. *See* U.S. TREASURY DEP'T, TAX REFORM STUDIES AND PROPOSALS, pt. 2, at 182-83, 91st Cong., 1st Sess. (Comm.

recommended by those sophisticated planners who have thought it through.[134] It seems to have become particularly popular among elite planners in New York City, where state and local taxes on top of federal levies push combined rates of death taxation to 75 percent[135] and combined income tax rates to 75.8 percent.[136] The rate trade-off there becomes an estate tax gain of $75 for every $24.20 sacrificed to charity, a deal which is difficult to resist.[137] Many New York planners indicated that use of the front-end trust for clients in the $10 million-plus category has become very common, if not the norm.[138]

Indeed, these New York planners advised that the technique is commonly used in the case of very large estates to eliminate the estate tax entirely.[139] Accomplishing this, as noted above, is simply a function of how high the annuity payout is set and the duration of the annuity period.[140] We were told by several of our interviewees that the favorite pattern which has evolved is the previously described annuity equal to 8 percent of the trust's original value for twenty-

---

Print 1969). At that time the Service's actuarial tables were based on a 3.5% discount factor, which unrealistically magnified the value of most annuities. *See* Treas. Reg. § 20.2031-7 (1970). The 1969 Tax Reform Act and modification of the actuarial tables in 1970 to shift to a 6% discount rate ended those halcyon days, and it has taken some time for planners to accommodate to the changes.

134. *See* Kartiganer, *Charitable Giving and Split Interest Trusts,* in PLI, ESTATE PLANNING FOR THE LARGE ESTATE 79-80 (1976); Moore, *Charitable Trusts,* in PLI, USE OF TRUSTS IN ESTATE PLANNING 119-21 (1976).

135. The New York estate tax goes to 21%, but because of the federal credit for a portion of state death taxes, the New York tax effectively adds only 5% to the federal burden in the highest brackets. *See* N.Y. TAX LAW § 952(a) (McKinney 1975); I.R.C. § 2011.

136. This rate is the combined effect of a state income tax rate of 15%, a city income tax rate of 4.3%, and the federal rate of 70%, with allowance for permitted deductibility. *See* N.Y. TAX LAW § 351 (McKinney 1975); N.Y. TAX LAW § 1304 (McKinney Supp. 1976); I.R.C. §§ 1, 164(a).

137. The real impetus came when, early in 1976, the top federal estate tax rate (under pre-1976 law) was 77% and a New York City estate tax with a top rate of 10.5% was enacted, making the combined city-state-federal estate tax as high as 92.5%. This city tax was repealed before becoming effective and the top federal rate has now been reduced to 70%, but the results of the thought processes which this combined burden stimulated linger on.

138. Thus one New York interviewee, when asked hypothetically what he might have done for Howard Hughes, responded without hesitation, "Well, I guess we would have rolled out the lead trust, wouldn't we?"

139. *See* sources cited in note 134 *supra.*

140. *See* Treas. Reg. § 20.2031-10. Table B (1970); Treas. Reg. § 25.2512-9, Table B (1958).

three to twenty-four years, which can easily be assured in the current market with high-grade, long-term corporate bonds, thus protecting the principal for the remaindermen without great effort. An alternative pattern, which gives the same deduction with greater investment freedom, is to fix the annuity somewhat lower and stretch out the trust longer. An annuity equal to 7 percent for thirty-three to thirty-four years will do the trick. One planner even suggested that he had established a front-end trust using a 6.5 percent annuity for forty-four years, for extremely wealthy clients whose major concern was the preservation of capital and freedom to manage it. Another planner said that he favored a 10 percent annuity for fifteen to sixteen years, on the theory that one can probably earn this amount, and even if not, it is better to eat up a little capital and get the trust terminated more quickly. In situations where a parent prefers not to inhibit his children with a long period of delay, he can commence a front-end trust during his life, so that by the time of his death all or most of the annuity period will have passed. This gives him the lifetime satisfactions of the charitable gift, and the charitable interest will fully offset any gift tax, enabling ultimate tax-free passage of the property to his children.[141]

In contrast to the abundance of activity in front-end trusts in New York, there seemed to be virtually no awareness of their potential outside that city. It is clear that the technique is only now catching on, and we may expect to see much growth in its use over the next few years, particularly because it is essentially unaffected by the Tax Reform Act.

141. One factor which discourages combinations producing a deduction equal to 100% of the trust principal is that front-end trusts which generate a deduction in excess of 60% of principal value are barred from holding a controlling interest in a business (as are all private foundations), while a trust generating a deduction of less than this percentage is free of this particular restraint. *See* I.R.C. § 4947(b)(3). Thus in some cases where it is desired to use a front-end trust as a receptacle for a closely held business, the annuity must be toned down.

CHAPTER THREE

Case Studies: How to Zero Base Budget for the Estate and Gift Tax

THE CASES ALREADY DISCUSSED provide good examples of how wealthy persons can avoid any serious transfer tax burden. Thus, we saw how a hypothetical millionaire with a typical family need do nothing more than undertake a simple gift-giving program to avoid most tax.[1] At a somewhat higher level we saw how Joseph E. Salsbury, who built up a business worth in excess of $13 million on his death, managed to pass it on to his children with a transfer tax payment of only a few hundred thousand dollars. This was an effective transfer tax rate of less than 5 percent, and was achieved by use of the preferred stock recapitalization technique and by judicious use of gifts early in the development of the business. It is an example that could be followed by any similarly situated businessman.

1. *See* ch. 2 text accompanying notes 75-77 *supra.*

The Salsbury Children

We did not mention earlier that Dr. Salsbury's son and daughter have continued in his tradition of effective estate planning, by taking full advantage of opportunities provided by the noncontrolling common stock.[2] They have given substantial amounts of this stock to their children (Dr. Salsbury's grandchildren) and have done so in years when the stock was of sufficiently low value to keep down the gift tax burden. By 1970, the last year for which we have data, the grandchildren of Dr. Salsbury, whose ages range from midtwenties to midthirties, owned almost 40 percent of the outstanding stock of the company. The total gift tax cost incurred in moving this stock to them was only $189,435. The seeds have thus been sown for continuation of this multimillion dollar business in family hands for yet another generation without significant transfer taxation.

Various tax avoidance techniques may be employed to pass on the remaining 60 percent of Salsbury Laboratories to this next generation even under the new law. There are eight grandchildren who, along with likely spouses and children of their own, provide a fertile route for tax-free exclusion gifts. Alternatively, if the business is about to expand into any new lines or geographic areas, it could consider doing so through the vehicle of a new corporation in which the grandchildren have dominant equity interests—on the Estée Lauder model mentioned earlier.[3] Control could be retained for the parents, if desired, through a special class of stock, as in the existing corporation. Depending on the nature of the business, other forms of business-diversion opportunities may also arise.

Another approach might be for the parents to create a personal holding company to take their remaining stock holdings as well as other assets and to set up that holding company with a dual-class stock structure similar to that of the existing corporation. They could then give the low-value common stock to their children. This would establish a two-tier dual stock situation, thereby combining the benefits achieved by Dr. Salsbury with the valuation erosion achieved by Paulina du Pont Dean and others. Still another alternative would be

2. The information in the text on the Salsbury family was developed from an analysis of data in the Tax Court record. *See* ch. 2 note 3 *supra.*

3. *See* ch. 2 text accompanying note 17 *supra.*

to make an installment sale of the remaining common stock to the children with low current payments and a balloon at the end. Or, if the parents have current charitable interests to be furthered, they might establish a front-end trust now which would eventually move the stock to their children. A ready vehicle for this front-end interest is the Dr. Joseph Salsbury Foundation, which has already been established and which held, as of 1967, 13 percent of the common stock. Each of these approaches has advantages and disadvantages, and some combination of them is probably recommended. All have as a common denominator the avoidance of much or all of the transfer tax burden.

The du Ponts

These illustrations indicate what can be done by persons of modest-to-substantial wealth to minimize transfer taxes. But, as we have observed, the real measure of the tax comes in the case of fabulous wealth, where the policy goals of the estate and gift tax are squarely put to a test. Fortunately for our purposes, there is sufficient data in court records on the du Pont family so that, with a little intelligent guesswork, we can reconstruct a case study of the passage of a major portion of that family fortune through three generations, which cover the entire period the estate and gift tax has been in effect. This case demonstrates how, in a not atypical situation of great wealth, the estate and gift tax has been reduced to a mere nuisance. It also provides a concrete example for exploring how difficult it will be for the current generation to continue effective tax avoidance after the 1976 Act.

Our study begins with William du Pont, Sr., the grandson of E.I. du Pont, who founded the du Pont Company in 1802, and the son of General Henry du Pont, who built the company to greatness with profits from Civil War munitions sales and the operation of the Gunpowder Trust in the 1870s and 1880s.[4] William was in direct line of descent to the du Pont fortune. At one time he was a major partner in the company (before its incorporation),[5] and, although he was cut off from much of its growth when control was transferred to a group of cousins in 1902, William retained a substantial interest in it as

4. M. DUKE, ch. 2 *supra* note 83, at 128-88.
5. *Id*. at 190-92.

well as other assets.[6] As a family chronicler says, "Willie would never want for money." [7]

Because his father died in 1889, before the days of transfer taxes, whatever wealth William inherited had never passed through the tax wringer. On his own death in 1928, William's estate was valued at $35.5 million.[8] In addition, he had made a series of gifts in trust to his son, daughter, daughter-in-law, and stepson in 1926 and 1927. The total value of securities transferred to these trusts was $6.4 million. Since there was no gift tax when these trusts were created, no transfer tax was payable on account of them.[9] An estate tax was payable on the property in William's estate, but because rates were lower then (the top rate was only 20 percent), the tax was only $6.4 million. Thus, William du Pont, Sr., holder of one of the largest fortunes in America (even today only a few hundred individuals, at most, have more than $40 million of wealth) and the first of his family line to die subject to the estate tax, surrendered only 15 percent of his wealth to transfer taxation in passing it on to his heirs. Even this amount was, as we shall see, probably the result of inadequate planning steps. The amount of tax was, in the year paid, almost 10 percent of all estate tax collections.[10]

The next generation, faced with a gift tax as well as steeply increased estate tax rates,[11] paradoxically has been even more successful in avoiding transfer taxes. Almost all the property of William, Sr., was left to his son, William, Jr., (Junior) and his daughter, Marion. A few parcels of real estate were left outright, and the balance, composing the bulk of the estate, was placed in a testamentary trust for these children, paying 60 percent of income to Junior and 40 percent to Marion.[12]

6. *Id*. at 223-36.

7. *Id*. at 231.

8. Delaware Trust Co. v. Handy, 53 F.2d 1042 (D. Del. 1931), provides the source for all the specific data in the text on the estate of William du Pont, Sr.

9. *Cf*. Handy v. Delaware Trust Co., 285 U.S. 352 (1932), *aff'g* 51 F.2d 867 (D. Del. 1931) (Wm. du Pont's gifts not taxable under estate tax contemplation of death rule). The gift tax was repealed as of January 1, 1926 and not reinstated until 1932.

10. Total estate tax collections in 1930, the year of du Pont's payment, were $64.8 million. *See* W. WARREN & S. SURREY, *supra* Intro. note 2, at 10.

11. The rates went up in the 1930s and were further increased to their maximum levels in 1941. *See* sources cited in Intro. note 2 *supra*.

12. *See* Last Will and Testament of William du Pont, Petitioner's Exhibit #15,

By the time of his death, on December 31, 1965, the son was wealthy beyond his father's probable expectations. The value of his interest in the testamentary trust created for him by his father was $242.4 million, and his interest in the trust created by gift from his father in 1926 was worth another $25–$50 million.[13] In addition, Junior held outright real estate, stocks and bonds, and other assets which his executor valued, net of debts and expenses of estate administration, at $22.4 million.[14] Thus, Junior's effective net worth at his death was indeed a princely sum—in round numbers, more than $300 million.

The son had engaged in very little estate-planning himself. He made no reportable gifts until 1961, when he was sixty-five years old. From 1961 to 1965 he made a total of $6.6 million in gifts, $3.2 million of which was charitable.[15] The noncharitable gifts followed no consistent pattern. In 1962 and 1963, Junior made aggressive use of the gift tax exclusion, making a series of $5,000-$6,000 gifts to a number of relatives. In other years, he made only modest use of this

in Estate of William du Pont, Jr., No. 2926-70, United States Tax Court. The will also provided for a series of annuities to other persons which are unimportant to this overall picture.

13. The value of the testamentary trust can be determined with precision because we know that the value of each one-fifth share distributed to Junior's children on March 28, 1966, was $48,488,894.51. *See* Answer of Defendants at ¶ 31, in Du Pont v. Delaware Trust Co., 310 A.2d 915 (Del. Ch. 1973), *rev'd,* 320 A.2d 694 (Del. 1974).

The value of the 1926 trust can be estimated from two bits of information: (1) the value of property transferred to the 1926 trust was approximately one-tenth of that placed in Junior's share of the testamentary trust, *see* Last Will and Testament of William du Pont, Petitioner's Exhibit #15, in Estate of William du Pont, Jr., No. 2926-70, United States Tax Court; Delaware Trust Co. v. Handy, 53 F.2d 1042 (D. Del. 1931), and (2) the accrued unpaid income of the 1926 trust as of Junior's death was approximately one-fifth that of the testamentary trust at the same time and there is reason to believe that both trusts were paying out income regularly. *See* estate tax return of William du Pont, Jr. at 17e, Petitioner's Exhibit #2, Estate of William du Pont, Jr., No. 2926-70, United States Tax Court. We have therefore valued the 1926 trust at one-fifth to one-tenth of the value of the testamentary trust.

14. This, and all data which follows in the text, is derived from the estate tax return and gift tax returns of William du Pont, Jr., filed as exhibits in Estate of William du Pont, Jr., No. 2926-70, United States Tax Court.

15. The major beneficiaries of this spurt of charitable activity were Delaware Park, Inc. (a racetrack), which received $2.23 million, and the State of Delaware, which received $463,000. One source reports that Delaware Park is operated by a du Pont controlled foundation and that, while all profits are to go to Delaware hospitals, the track was operating at a loss in 1970. J. PHELAN & R. POZEN, THE COMPANY STATE 346-47 (1973).

opportunity. In total, approximately $200,000 was disposed of in exclusion gifts. An additional $1.8 million was put in trusts for family friends and employees.[16] Finally, Junior made gifts in trust to his children of two pieces of real property, a ranch near Palm Springs, California (value $100,000), and a 242-acre horse farm in Delaware, which consisted of all the property surrounding the house in which he and his wife lived (value $1.1 million). With regard to both these gifts of real estate, Junior leased the property back and continued to be lessee with full rights of use and occupancy at the time of his death.[17]

Some of this appears to be a modest attempt at estate tax reduction through gift-giving, but most of the amounts involved were too small to have made a dent in a fortune this size. The single largest noncharitable gift in dollar value, that of the 242 acres surrounding his own house, appears to have been motivated by estate tax avoidance motives, in view of the location of the property and the leaseback arrangements. The Internal Revenue Service succeeded in taxing this property to Junior's estate under recapture provisions of the tax code.[18]

All of this, however, was trifling compared to the most important item in Junior's estate plan, an item which he did not have to lift a finger to get. Both the 1926 lifetime trust and the 1928 testamentary trust created by William, Sr., were generation-skipping trusts and thus were entirely free of transfer taxation to Junior's generation. These trusts were early versions of generation-skipping trusts and did not give the son the broad powers of appointment commonly included in more recent trusts. Nonetheless in addition to receiving all

16. William, Jr. funded a trust for his grandchildren ($245,000), a pension plan for his employees ($564,000), a trust for Alice Marble ($179,000), and a trust for his then wife, Margaret Osborne du Pont ($800,000), whom he divorced shortly thereafter.

17. One other estate-planning mechanism which we discussed earlier may have been used by Mr. du Pont. The major item in the portfolio of stock which he owned outright ($8.4 million of a total of $23.5 million) was stock in Shapdale, Inc., a closely held holding company. The Internal Revenue Service succeeded in raising the taxable value of this to $9 million, but if our findings regarding valuation discounts received on such stock are accurate, it may well be that the real value of the Shapdale, Inc., stock was millions more, possibly double the value indicated.

18. Estate of William du Pont, Jr., 63 T.C. 746 (1975). A well-designed installment sale with leaseback would probably have been much more effective for Mr. du Pont. He should have talked with Mr. Hudspeth. *See* ch. 2 text accompanying notes 21-35 *supra*.

the income from his shares of these trusts, amounting to millions of dollars annually, Junior had effective control over the trust property during his lifetime because he was president, chairman of the board of directors, and controlling shareholder in the bank that was trustee of the trusts.

The end result is that Junior paid a total estate tax of $17.4 million and earlier had paid gift taxes on behalf of himself and his wife estimated at $0.5 million to $1 million, making his total transfer tax burden roughly $18 million. This is a sizable sum when compared to the wealth of $30–$40 million which Junior owned outright and passed on to his heirs. But when compared to his real wealth of more than $300 million, this tax burden can be put in perspective. It is approximately 6 percent of that total wealth, which can fairly be described as the nuisance tax level.

This carries the family fortune to the present generation of Junior's five children, Jean, Evelyn, Henry, John, and William III, whose ages range from midtwenties to midfifties. These children not only succeeded to their father's wealth but also will receive on the death of their Aunt Marion her share of the inheritance from William, Sr. (she having no children).[19] Rather than attempt false precision about the sum of these inheritances, let us simply say that each of these individuals must concern himself or herself with planning for an estate worth more than $100 million at 1966 values,[20] and if all goes moderately well, is likely to be worth several times that by the time of his or her death. These are among the few largest fortunes in the United States. This vast wealth is not attributable to any pro-

19. Du Pont v. Delaware Trust Co., 310 A.2d 915, 917 (Del. Ch. 1973), *rev'd,* 320 A.2d 694 (Del. 1974).

20. Upon William, Jr.'s death, his share of William, Sr.'s testamentary trust was distributed equally among these children, each receiving $48.5 million. *See* note 13 *supra.* On the probable assumption that the 1926 lifetime trust was similarly distributed and that these children have acquired modest additional wealth from other sources, each of these children had wealth of at least $60 million as of 1966. In addition, the one-fifth shares of their aunt's interest in the 1928 testamentary trust which each will receive will add an additional $32 million to each of their estates (using 1966 values). Since this is the remainder of a generation-skipping trust, it will bear no tax. It is also likely that these children will succeed to shares of trusts created in 1926 for their aunt, which will deposit another several million or even tens of millions on them. The principal placed in the 1926 trust created for their aunt was even greater than that of their father's 1926 trust. *See* Delaware Trust Co. v. Handy, 53 F.2d 1042 (D. Del. 1931) ($3.3 million as compared to $2 million, as of 1926).

ductive activity by any of its current owners who simply inherited it, nor necessarily to activity of their father or grandfather. Rather, the core of the fortune dates back to their great-grandfather's earnings during the heyday of aggressive and unchecked capitalism, and the remainder could well be the natural accumulation that can be expected when a large sum is kept invested for decades at a relatively low rate of current return and accordingly high rate of capital appreciation.[21] Transfer taxes have been, despite the death of two generations during the period that such taxes have been in effect, largely irrelevant to the accumulation and current holding of this sum.

But is the current generation the one that must face the transfer tax moment of truth? The wealth we have described came to its current holders free of trust since they are a generation at the end of a skipping trust. If this generation of children does nothing about estate planning, it is not unreasonable to expect that the estate of each, worth $100 million at 1966 values, will be worth, say, $300 million by the time of death, and will bear an estate tax of $210 million. Can they reduce this burden substantially? The answer is yes, using the techniques we have discussed and a dose of cleverness. The only real dilemma facing these du Pont scions is in deciding where and how the riches should go. This can be a serious problem for those who either do not have children or, heeding the warnings of Andrew Carnegie, do not want to inundate their heirs with wealth, but let us assume that such philosophical problems are not a concern.

Rather, let us assume that the five children of William du Pont, Jr., have offspring and wish to pass the maximum wealth to them and their children to preserve and enhance the dynasty for generations yet to come. What might a good estate planner advise one of these du Ponts to do? There are many possibilities and we can only speculate, but the following is one conceivable plan. (In addition to the textual discussion which follows, the structure of this plan for one child, William III, is illustrated in figure 3-1.)

21. The appreciation of du Pont Company stock between 1928 when William, Sr., died and 1965, when William, Jr., died, was greater than the increase in the family fortune during that period. A share of du Pont stock, which sold for $256 in 1927 (mean value) was worth $3,404 in 1965 (mean value, allowing for splits) and the holder would also own 1.36 shares of General Motors stock (received as a divestiture dividend in antitrust settlement), which was worth $139 in 1965 (mean value). The aggregate value in 1965, $3,543, is almost fourteen times the value in 1927. By comparison, the property placed in trust by William, Sr., increased in value by less than twelve times.

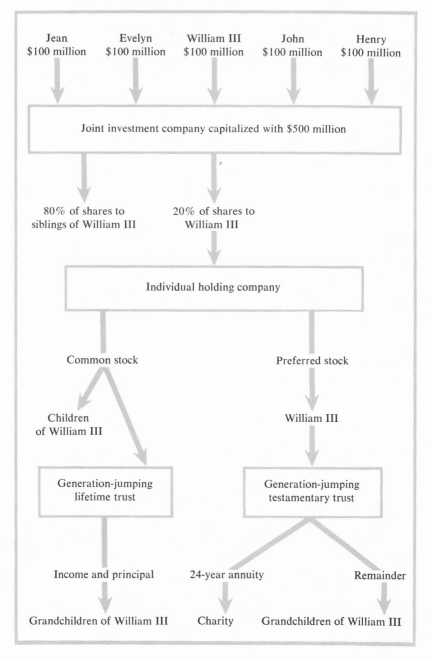

Figure 3-1. Hypothetical Estate Plan for William du Pont III

Obtain Valuation Discounts

The first step is to transfer all assets, or as much as each child is willing to surrender, to a holding company formed to act as a joint investment vehicle for this group of children. There could be difficulties in obtaining the necessary cooperation to establish this company, because there was intersibling rivalry in estate litigation following the death of Junior.[22] However, the nontax advantages of having such an investment vehicle, coupled with the 40 percent to 50 percent discount in estate and gift tax values, which it would be expected to produce for the holders of each minority interest in this closely held family company, might be enough to overcome objections. After all, use of family investment companies is an old du Pont tradition, as we have already seen.[23] The past history of rivalry would provide valuable ammunition in arguing that the minority lack of control is meaningful. Assuming that each child transferred the bulk of his assets to this new corporation when the assets were worth $100 million, the estate of each could be reduced immediately to as little as $50 to $60 million. What will have happened to the other $40 to $50 million? Nothing. It remains there producing income, power, and security for the du Pont children. They can retrieve it through corporate distributions whenever a majority of them choose to do so.[24] They know where it is. Only the tax law has lost track of it.

Freeze Estate Values

After the taxable value of these wealth holdings has been reduced by minority discounts, each child could transfer his stock of the joint investment company to a separate individual holding company, along with other personal assets, art collections, hobby businesses and other property which it was not thought suitable to put in the joint company. This separate holding company should have two classes of stock, as with *Salsbury*. The preferred stock, embodying all current value, can be retained by the child creating the holding company, but

22. *See* du Pont v. Delaware Trust Co., 310 A.2d 915, 919 (Del. Ch. 1973), *rev'd*, 320 A.2d 684 (Del. 1974).

23. *See* Paulina du Pont Dean, 19 Tax Ct. Mem. Dec. 281 (1960). *See also* Mary A.B. du Pont Laird, 38 B.T.A. 926 (1938).

24. Such distributions require some planning to avoid income tax problems, but they can be managed. *See* sources cited in ch. 2 note 111 *supra*.

the low-value common stock should promptly be given. Some of this common stock can be given outright or in trust to the donor's children, with the idea of beginning a principal fund to protect the next succeeding generation, and the balance placed in a generation-jumping trust for the benefit of the donor's grandchildren. (Of course, if this plan had been put into effect a year ago, a generation-skipping trust could have been used, possibly even in perpetuity, and would have remained valid.)

This process accomplishes the dual goals of freezing the taxable value of the current generation's holdings and assuring that much of the growth embodied in this new stock will escape tax for at least one more generation. In addition, because it imposes another corporate layer on ownership of underlying assets it adds another argument for valuation discount. This argument will be undercut by the fact that only preferred stock is retained, and this stock tends to have a more secure value than common stock, but depending on the rights of the preferred stock and the earnings of the corporation, some discount might be obtained. In any event, it would not be unreasonable to anticipate that the holdings of each child will likely have been reduced from the original $100 million coupled with an expectation of future appreciation of much more, to only $50 million, shorn of future appreciation. Not a penny of transfer tax has yet been incurred.

Neutralize Tax on Remaining Assets

The controlling preferred stock which each child still holds will presumably be drawing down the full annual earnings produced by the original $100 million contribution to the joint investment company, which, assuming a low rate of return, say 4 percent, will be producing annual after-tax income of little more than $1 million annually. The clients will probably want this sum to live on, so no further lifetime gift-giving should be contemplated. There are, however, a variety of ways in which this remaining stock interest can escape estate tax.

Assuming that the common stock interests given to children and grandchildren under step two matures into assets with sufficient value to provide a proper standard of living for those persons, a testamentary front-end charitable trust would work spectacularly as a means of handling the preferred stock.[25] Each child could bequeath his interest to a trust paying a $4 million annual charitable annuity for twenty-four years. This sum is the amount which the stock is presumably earning. Although it is only a 4 percent return on the original investment of $100 million, it is an 8 percent return on the discounted value of the property now in the child's estate and thus produces a deduction equal to the full $50 million estate tax value of the property. There is in other words, a symbiosis between the valuation discount and the front-end trust, which enables our client to avoid estate taxation completely while effectively paying the charity a twenty-four-year annuity equal to only 4 percent of the real value of the underlying assets.[26] The remaining interest in this front-end trust would, of course, be paid directly to the donor's grandchildren, so that in twenty-four years the family would own all the property and would have few estate-planning worries until the death of William, Sr.'s, great-great-grandchildren, sometime in the twenty-first or even the twenty-second century.[27]

The total estate and gift tax burden of this plan? Zero. The total surrender of income or property during life by our client? There is (1) a transfer to heirs of income produced by future growth of property and (2) a loss of direct ownership of property. However, all

25. The restrictions on excess business holdings by a front-end trust raise no problems because stock in a passive investment company rather than an active business is being contributed. *See* I.R.C. § 4943(d)(4).

26. The risk in this scheme is that it depends on obtaining a full 50% discount from the underlying asset value of the joint investment company in valuing a child's preferred stock in his or her holding company. If a discount of lesser amount is obtained, and the charitable annuity remains fixed at $4 million per year, the annuity will not yield a deduction large enough to cover the full value of the property. A discount of only 30%, for example, producing a value of $70 million for the preferred stock, would leave $20 million to be taxed in excess of the $50 million deduction for the annuity. The perfect system to avoid this risk would be to make the annuity amount a fixed percentage (8%) of the estate tax valuation actually determined for the preferred stock. Then, if the discount is 50% and the valuation $50 million, the annuity will be $4 million as planned. If the discount is only 30% and the valuation $70 million, then the annuity will be $5.6 million producing the needed increase in the deduction. Wonder of wonders, the Regulations specifically authorize a front-end annuity determined in precisely this fashion. Treas. Reg. § 20.2055-2(e)(2)(v) (1974).

27. Three of the five current children are old enough to have grandchildren already. If they do have grandchildren, they can route some property to a group even further removed from the likely date of taxation.

income from the original property is retained and effective voting control over all property (including future growth) is maintained. The ultimate diversion of income or property from heirs of our client at death? There is a temporary, twenty-four-year diversion of a portion of the income from the original property. That is all, and even that goes to a charity or charities selected by the client.

A key aspect of the foregoing plan is the creation of a joint family investment company, producing a substantial valuation discount. What if the necessary cooperation could not be obtained or if one of the children chose not to participate? It might be possible to achieve the same objective by dividing ownership and control of an investment company among a child, his spouse, and his children. But if this too is not feasible, what might an estate planner then advise?

One possibility would be to pursue the plan described above but without the initial step. The problem is that because the value of the retained preferred stock will not have been deeply discounted through the mechanism of an underlying joint investment company, it would be necessary to pay a larger annual sum to charity (possibly close to a full $8 million) or to stretch out the annuity for a period longer than twenty-four years. Those burdens might well be manageable and worthwhile in light of the benefits obtained. If desired, however, the simplest way to mitigate these burdens would be to split up ownership of the preferred stock so that it is not all held by the child who created the holding company.

The child could, for example, transfer one-half of this preferred stock to the generation-jumping lifetime trust in return for a private annuity and the other half to a separate lifetime front-end trust paying an annuity to charity for the life of the child.[28] The annuity payments would be determined under Internal Revenue Service tables, based on the valuation of the stock transferred and the life expectancy of the child. Since a minority interest in a closely held investment company is the property being transferred to each trust, it should be expected that a significant valuation discount could be obtained that would reduce the amount of annuity needed. For example, for a forty-nine-year-old man (such as Henry du Pont, who

28. The Regulations specifically permit a person's life rather than a fixed term to be the measuring period for a front-end annuity. Treas. Reg. § 25-2522(c)(2)(v) (1975).

initiated the litigation over his father's estate and is therefore least likely to opt for the joint investment company), a life annuity of $3.25 million per year is worth roughly $37.5 million.[29] If a 25 percent discount can be anticipated on property transferred to pay for the annuity, $50 million of stock with a discounted value of $37.5 million could be transferred in fair exchange for a $3.25 million annuity. Here again, the valuation discount, in effect, gives the taxpayer an edge to beat the annuity tables and makes both the private annuity and the charitable annuity more attractive as estate-planning devices. The end result of this scheme, as with other plans discussed, is no estate or gift tax. However, there is no direct legal precedent for the means used to gain a valuation discount here (dividing stock interests between a charitable trust and a noncharitable trust paying a private annuity), and it is therefore less secure than the technique of establishing a joint investment company.

All these plans are, obviously, rather extreme proposals designed to demonstrate that zero-base budgeting for the estate tax is a reasonable starting point for any person with serious estate tax avoidance designs. However, as this lengthy discussion should have demonstrated, the essential elements of these proposals, as well as the prior plans actually used by the du Ponts, are standard planning practices for the very wealthy. Thus, for example, the idea of a pooled investment vehicle which is so central to our proposal is not only an established procedure in the du Pont family but is also used by the Rockefellers.[30] The Rockefellers likewise have made extensive use of generation-skipping trusts, many of which will remain in effect for another generation after the death of Nelson and his brothers and will not be subject to estate tax until the generation of Nelson's children die.[31] The proposals we make for the current generation of du Ponts, while seemingly elaborate to those unaccustomed to great fortunes, are not really more complicated and do not really require

29. *See* Treas. Reg. § 25.2512-9(e), Table A(1) (1970).

30. *See Nomination of Nelson A. Rockefeller to be Vice-President of the United States: Hearings Before the House Comm. on the Judiciary* 93d Cong., 2d Sess. 224, 775, 847 (1974).

31. *See Nomination of Nelson A. Rockefeller to be Vice-President of the United States: Hearings Before the Senate Comm. on Rules and Admin.*, 93d Cong., 2d Sess. 45 (1974); P. COLLIER & D. HOROWITZ, THE ROCKEFELLERS, AN AMERICAN DYNASTY 204, 625 (1976).

any greater surrender of personal control over property than has long been customary in such families.

In actual practice, of course, clients would undoubtedly be less than totally committed to saving taxes for the benefit of prospective heirs. They would surely wish to retain some assets free of trusts or corporations, and those assets would be exposed to the estate tax. But, as the man said, it's a voluntary tax, and the amount left so exposed is up to the client.

CHAPTER FOUR

Reform Possibilities

CLEARLY, THE ESTATE AND GIFT TAX is not striking terror into the hearts of the very wealthy, nor is it even seriously burdening most persons who devote effort to avoidance. Everyone does not fully exploit the tax avoidance opportunities, it is true. But we can gain little reassurance from this failure of action. Those who remain burdened by the tax include those who reject tax avoidance for reasons of principle, those who give low priority to engaging in complicated maneuvers solely for tax purposes, those who have no natural alternative to the government for disposition of their fortunes (presumably because they do not have children, do not trust those that they do have, or do not want to burden them with great wealth), and those who die inopportunely.

There are, in addition, some very wealthy individuals who, because of the nature or amount of their asset holdings, cannot easily take advantage of opportunities theoretically available to them. There is an awkward gap in estate planning between the relatively simple techniques that suffice for those with a million dollars or less and the elaborate structures suitable for the du Ponts and other megamillionaires. For someone with accumulated wealth of, say $3 million to $5 million, estate-freezing will work well, but it may be

difficult to dispose of the accumulation because the individual may
not be able to afford to tie up a major portion of his or her wealth in
such devices as front-end trusts. If an individual in this category is of
advanced age and is no longer active in business affairs, such that
substantial future growth of asset values is problematic, even estate-
freezing strategies may provide little solace. For such a "too little,
too late" person, the tax bite can be reduced substantially but maybe
not down to the nuisance level.

This group of tax-bearing persons, selected by a combination of
high principle and odd luck and including such notable specimens
as Howard Hughes, surely evokes public curiosity and, in various
instances, sympathy, respect, or hostility. But it is difficult to imagine
any national public policy that can justify singling this group out for
the burdens of a steeply progressive tax, with rates going to 70 percent, which is not visited upon their equally or more wealthy com-
patriots who have lower principles or better luck.

Moreover, the estate tax avoidance engaged in by those who do
not pay the tax rarely possesses the mitigating features that sometimes make income tax avoidance at least arguably tolerable. In
many major instances of income tax avoidance the free market provides an inherent limitation on excessive exploitation in that the tax
benefits from income tax shelter investments often become factored
into the price of the investments. In other words, there is a finite
supply of good income tax shelter investment opportunities, and as
more tax avoiders attempt to exploit the tax benefits inherent in a
particular shelter, they are likely to be driven to more and more
marginal opportunities and eventually to be driven away from that
shelter.[1] In addition, there is a substantial tendency for the pursuit
of income tax avoidance to direct investors into areas preferred by
Congress. This is certainly true of real estate investments and pur-
chases of state and local bonds, and it may be advanced as a partial
justification for the income tax benefits extended to oil investments

1. *See* Bittker, *Tax Shelters and Tax Capitalization or Does the Early Bird Get a
Free Lunch?* 28 NAT'L TAX J. 416 (1975). This inherent adjustment is never complete because the tax factor in the price of an investment will normally reflect the
tax benefit available to the lowest marginal-bracket investor using the shelter. Those
in higher brackets receive a windfall. This upper-bracket windfall is the reason the
aggregate benefit received by states and municipalities in the form of lower borrow-
ing costs because of the exemption of their bond interest is less than aggregate lost
revenues to the federal government.

and to all capital gains income. Without getting into an argument about the desirability of income tax incentives in general or of any particular incentive, we can observe that there may be at least some by-product societal benefit from the existence of many income tax avoidance opportunities.

By contrast, the estate tax avoidance mechanisms discussed in this book are for the most part neither self-limiting nor the providers of by-product societal benefits. They are not self-limiting because they do not involve a finite supply of opportunities. When one family corporation undertakes a recapitalization, it in no way limits the opportunity or raises the cost for anyone else to do so. When one wealthy family establishes a personal holding company to obtain valuation discounts, it in no way discourages anyone else from doing so. Estate tax avoidance does not provide by-product societal benefits, because it involves manipulations in the form of property ownership more than any choice of particular investment opportunities. There are exceptions, of course, to this generalization. Most notably, the use of charitable front-end trusts and the use of gifts of conservation easements provide rather obvious public benefits. These exceptions do not undercut the overall accuracy of the generalization, however: most estate tax avoidance produces very little good for anyone.

Coupled with this absence of positive benefit are the undesirable by-products of estate tax avoidance. The avoidance process greatly encourages the tying up of property in trusts and holding companies. Worst of all, it offers strong inducement to reconcentrate aggregations of wealth that have strayed into independent hands, as we saw in our discussion of the proposed new joint investment company for the du Pont children.

It is sometimes suggested that estate tax avoidance has positive benefits because it facilitates the continued holding of family businesses (such as Salsbury Laboratories) in family hands, without the need to sell shares to pay taxes. This is not really an argument on behalf of avoidance, however. It is rather an argument against harsh imposition of the estate tax in such situations. If there is a desire not to impose unreasonable burdens on small businesses, there should be a direct protective mechanism (such as the existing provisions permitting deferrals of tax payments),[2] not a system which forces such

2. *See* new I.R.C. §§ 6163, 6166. *See also* new I.R.C. § 2032A.

businesses to contort themselves with strange capital structures so as to avoid taxation, and which imposes a stern tax on the unwary.

In sum, because estate tax avoidance is such a successful and yet wasteful process, one suspects that the present estate and gift tax serves no purpose other than to give reassurance to the millions of unwealthy that entrenched wealth is being attacked. The attack is, however, more cosmetic than real and the economy is paying the price of fettered capital and distorted property ownership for this tax cosmetology. Unless the system can be significantly reformed, consideration should be given to scrapping it or at least replacing it with a more effective means of accomplishing its perceived goals.

Current Reform Proposals

The Tax Reform Act of 1976 adopted most recent major reform proposals,[3] including those made by the Treasury Department in 1969.[4] Those reforms are important, but as we have seen, the changes are unlikely to have much effect in increasing tax liabilities.[5] Most of the traditional avoidance mechanisms are not even affected.

It is not clear what, if any, further reform steps are even being contemplated today. One possibility is an actual tax at death on accrued capital gains. The failure to impose such a tax is the most significant deviation in the 1976 Act from prior reform proposals. However, if, as we have suggested, the newly enacted carryover basis rule actually worsens the estate tax avoidance problem by undercutting the former stepped-up-basis reward for holding property, the imposition of an actual tax at death will cause taxpayers to turn to estate tax avoidance with a newfound enthusiasm. This is not to say that a capital gains tax at death is not justified on grounds of income tax equity—it clearly is—but rather that it is more likely to be a negative than a positive factor on the estate tax avoidance front.

3. *See* G. BREAK & J. PECHMAN, FEDERAL TAX REFORM, THE IMPOSSIBLE DREAM? 110-11 (1975).

4. U.S. TREASURY DEP'T, TAX REFORM STUDIES AND PROPOSALS, 91st Cong., 1st Sess., pt. 3, at 331-409 (Comm. Print 1969).

5. The revenue estimates for the antiavoidance reforms, which we suspect are based on more optimistic assumptions than those in this book, nonetheless show only negligible revenue gains. *See* STAFF OF JOINT COMM. ON TAXATION, SUMMARY OF THE TAX REFORM ACT OF 1976, at 114 (1976).

Another statutory change attracting the attention of reformers, which might make sense under the income tax but which would aggravate estate and gift tax problems, is corporate-individual income tax integration. If the corporate "double tax" were ended, a major deterrent to the creation of personal holding companies would thereby be eliminated. We should then be prepared to expect much more use of holding companies as repositories for wealth to gain the advantages of future growth diversions through dual-stock capital structures and valuation reductions through minority interest and marketability discounts.

Present reform proposals thus give more, not less, reason to be concerned about the avoidance mechanisms described.

Better Enforcement of Existing Law

Some modest improvement of the current situation might be obtained with more aggressive enforcement of the existing law.

Thus, for example, the *Salsbury*-type recapitalization would be more difficult to carry off successfully if the Internal Revenue Service were stricter in its valuation of the common stock interests. Common stock in a corporation, even if current earnings and assets are inadequate to offer anything to the stock, clearly has substantial value if there is reason to anticipate future corporate growth. The common stock in such a situation can be likened to a stock option with the option price fixed equal to the current market price. While such an option can produce no immediate cash benefit for its holder, the long-term value is indisputable. However, this observation having been made, it must be admitted that the potential for much success from applying this theory is not great. For one thing, the problems of collecting a full tax on compensatory options have long plagued the income tax.[6] Moreover, in *Salsbury*-type cases, the value of the option embodied in the common stock is usually dependent on the goodwill of a parent who dominates the closely held corporation. So long as his children continue to own the stock, that stock is a good bet because of the parent's likely benign disposition toward them. No stranger can depend very much on this disposition, however, and as a

6. *See* 1 S. SURREY, W. WARREN, P. McDANIEL & H. AULT, FEDERAL INCOME TAXATION 1083-1100 (1972).

consequence the stock would do very poorly on the open market. This is an interesting irony in estate and gift tax avoidance. The continuing corporate control by the parent through his management and voting power in the corporation is a desired aspect of the basic avoidance scheme and in a sense increases the value to his children of what he has given. But it also has the secondary benefit of reducing the market value of the gift.

The valuation difficulties posed by the parent's retained control might justify the Internal Revenue Service in taking an entirely different tack in such cases. The Service could take the position that no taxable gift has been made—and thus no valuation is necessary—until the actual value of the gift to the children becomes more firmly and more clearly established, as on the sale of the stock or the death of the parent. There is some precedent under the gift tax for deferring the date of taxability because of valuation uncertainties,[7] and even more precedent under the income tax law, particularly in the somewhat analogous area of stock options.[8] As in those other cases, the process of deferral here greatly improves the possibility of obtaining significant tax revenue. The idea of deferring taxation until valuation is more feasible also seems well suited to dealing with the problems raised by survivorship benefit plans,[9] and since the valuation process can be so extraordinarily difficult in such instances, the Service might expect some degree of responsiveness from the courts.

Other valuation problems might also respond to new Internal Revenue Service enforcement efforts. The notion that the Service acquiesces in 25 percent to 50 percent discounts on stock of personal holding companies owned within a narrow family group is shocking. In deference to the Service, it must be conceded that attempts to resist such discounts have not met with much success in the lower courts, but the issue has never been appealed by the government to a higher court.[10] There is a reasonable chance that, if properly framed, this issue might receive sympathetic treatment on appeal.

7. *See* Rev. Rul. 69-346, 1969-1 C.B. 227; Rev. Rul. 73-61, 1973-1 C.B. 408. *See also* ALI, FEDERAL ESTATE AND GIFT TAXATION RECOMMENDATIONS ADOPTED BY THE ALI AND REPORTERS' STUDIES 22-23 (1969) (discussing a "wait and see" approach for dealing with difficulties in charitable valuations).

8. *See* Burnett v. Logan, 283 U.S. 404 (1931); materials cited in note 6 *supra*.

9. *See* ch. 2 text accompanying notes 71-74 *supra*.

10. Indeed, our research discloses more than 60 cases involving valuation dis-

The absence of appeals may be the result of viewing these cases as simple factual disputes about valuation, which are not thought to be the proper grist for the appeal process. That perception is plainly wrong. The problem in the valuation discount cases is not so much an erroneous construction of the facts as the application of wrong-headed basic principles. The root of the problem is that the courts persist in the notion that the proper approach to valuation is to hypothesize what strangers on the open market would pay for property. In so doing, the courts fail to give adequate recognition to the value of the property to the particular persons involved in light of their peculiar circumstances and in view of the goals and purposes of the estate and gift taxes. The open market approach to valuation is not demanded by the tax statute which in general speaks of the value of property,[11] and an alternative, more personalized approach seems preferable.

Thus in the case of lifetime gifts of minority interests by a parent who owns a controlling interest in the same property, it is questionable whether a minority discount should ever be allowed. A fundamental purpose of the gift tax is to protect against lifetime erosions of the estate tax base.[12] That purpose is better served if we look to the value of property in the hands of the parent, to see how much his wealth has been reduced by the gift, than if we look at its value in other hands and allow the parent's voluntary, gratuitous creation of a

---

counts and only five such appeals since 1950. Four were appeals by the taxpayer. *See* Silverman v. Commissioner, 538 F.2d 977 (2d Cir. 1976); Snyder v. United States, 182 F. Supp. 71 (W.D.N.C. 1960), *rev'd,* 285 F.2d 857 (4th Cir. 1961); Estate of Alvin Thalheimer, 33 T.C.M. (CCH) 877 (1974), *aff'd,* 532 F.2d 751 (4th Cir.), *cert. denied,* 97 S. Ct. 317 (1976); William Hamm, Jr., 20 T.C.M. (CCH) 1814 (1961), *aff'd,* 325 F.2d 934 (8th Cir. 1963), *cert. denied,* 377 U.S. 993 (1964). The one government appeal raised only narrow, specialized questions and did not go to the basic problems discussed in the text. Louis v. United States, 66-1 U.S. Tax Cas. ¶ 12,360 (N.D. Ill. 1965), *aff'd,* 369 F.2d 263 (7th Cir. 1966). In the past 10 years the government has never appealed.

11. *See* I.R.C. §§ 2031, 2512. I.R.C. § 2031(b) adds the requirement that in cases of unlisted stock the prices of similar traded securities must be taken into account in the valuation process, "in addition to all other factors." This provision lends some support to the open market approach taken by the courts, but it hardly dictates that approach. *Cf.* Rothgery v. United States, 475 F.2d 591 (Ct. Cl. 1973) (rejecting search for hypothetical outside buyer when recipient himself was likely buyer).

12. Sanford v. Commissioner, 308 U.S. 39, 44 (1939).

minority interest to give him a transfer tax windfall.[13] In estate tax situations, the property is valued according to what the decedent owned, without taking account of any lesser value the property may have in the hands of recipients, even in situations where a controlling block of stock is split into minority interests by bequests. A good argument can be made that the gift tax ought to take the same approach. There is precedent elsewhere in gift tax law for using the loss in value to the donor to determine gift values. Thus, it is well established that the gift of a life estate is valued by taking an actuarially determined multiple of the underlying value of the property involved, even in cases where it is most unlikely that the life estate could be sold to a stranger for this price. Life estates measured by the lives of other people simply are not appealing assets to put on the market, but they clearly reduce the donor's wealth by the actuarial multiple. The established valuation procedure effectively takes that fact into account. To the extent that the property interest created by the donor is worth less on the open market than the amount taxed to him, his choice was voluntary and need not generate concern.[14] The adoption of a new combined estate and gift tax in the 1976 Act provides further justification for this approach of valuing gifts by looking to the extent the estate tax base has been eroded, and the Service might well use the new law as a ground for toughening its policies in this respect.

Moreover, for both estate and gift tax purposes, in situations where an individual donor or decedent himself owns no more than a minority interest in property, courts should take account of his relationship to other shareholders and the corporate management in determining the extent to which the individual involved actually is burdened by being a minority shareholder.[15] In considering discounts

13. *Cf.* Feld, *supra* ch. 2 note 95, at 944-45 (suggesting avoidance windfall under present rules).

14. The approach recommended in the text is also supported by the well-known case of Guggenheim v. Rasquin, 312 U.S. 254 (1941). In that case a taxpayer purchased a single premium insurance policy for $800,000. The cash surrender value of the policy was only $700,000. She promptly gave the policy away, and was held to have made a gift of $800,000 rather than the $700,000 cash value. *Cf.* United States v. Allen, 293 F.2d 916 (10th Cir.), *cert. denied*, 368 U.S. 944 (1961) (same approach adopted in interpreting and applying the "gift in contemplation of death" provision).

15. This is similar to the suggestion of Professor Feld who would limit it, however, to a presumption against the donor rather than an absolute rule. *See* Feld, *supra* ch. 2 note 95 at 945-46.

for marketability and expenses on sale of property, courts should consider whether sale is actually contemplated and, if so, whether the supposed burdens fall upon the individuals involved, assuming that they will follow the least costly and burdensome procedures available for sale. There is some precedent for this approach in the retention value doctrine, which has received a modicum of judicial approval in some closely held corporation valuation situations.[16] The doctrine needs substantial expansion and elaboration, however, if it is to have much significance in altering the scandalous state of valuation discounts.

Another approach to restraining valuation maneuvers might be to attack certain transactions, such as the transfer of property to a holding company, as shams that ought to be ignored for tax purposes. The sham transaction doctrine is a sleeping giant in the enforcement arsenal which has in the past been aroused on odd occasions,[17] and certain valuation cases are situations where it might be properly invoked. Some of the other avoidance techniques discussed, especially the use of installment sales, also seem vulnerable to challenge under the sham transaction doctrine. However, the Service did present that argument in the installment sale cases discussed earlier, without success. Some installment sale cases might also be amenable to an aggressive attack under the retained income and control doctrines of sections 2036 and 2038, if the bona fide sale exception in those sections could be negated with a sham argument.[18]

Another innovative approach that could be used to attack the initial incorporation of a joint holding company, such as that proposed

16. *See* Rothgery v. United States, 475 F.2d 591, 594 (Ct. Cl. 1974); Estate of Pearl Gibbons Reynolds, 55 T.C. 172 (1970).

17. *See, e.g.,* Marvin M. May, 31 T.C.M. (CCH) 279 (1972); Leonard Marcus, 30 T.C.M. (CCH) 1263 (1971), both of which were recently cited by the Joint Committee on Internal Revenue Taxation as suggesting a sham transaction attack on certain aspects of income tax shelter deals in JT. COMM. ON INTERNAL REVENUE TAX SHELTERS: MOVIE FILMS 6 (Comm. Print 1975) (prepared for the use of the Committee on Ways and Means).

18. There are other, narrower, litigative challenges which might also be considered. The Service should challenge any recognition of a discount for latent capital gains taxes in situations where the basis step-up on death can be used to abate that tax. The Service has had some success in at least one case arguing that minority discounts should be reduced to take account of the fact that majority shareholders in a corporation have a fiduciary duty to minority shareholders, protecting the latter against more extreme exploitation of their interest. *See* Seymour Silverman, 33 T.C.M. (CCH) 1321 (1974), *aff'd,* 538 F.2d 927 (2d Cir. 1976). This concept might be expanded.

for the du Pont children, might be to argue that in such cases the value that disappears is, in effect, a gift to the corporation subject to gift tax at the time the corporation is created. It is clear that, where one shareholder in a corporation makes a contribution to the corporation's capital and does not receive a compensating increase in his stock interest in return, he will be deemed to have made a gift to other shareholders to the extent of their pro rata interests in the newly contributed property.[19] It would not be out of the question to carry this doctrine an additional step and say that, even where other shareholders do not get any windfall, if a contributing shareholder receives stock that is in fact worth less than his contributed property (because of the minority discount or otherwise), he has made a taxable gift.[20] This is simply an extension of the loss to the donor theory of measuring gifts proposed above.

The difficulty with all these approaches is that their ultimate success depends on the courts, and the courts at all levels have in recent years shown themselves notably insensitive to the needs of sound estate and gift tax administration. The decision of the Supreme Court in *United States v. Byrum*[21] is perhaps the most notorious example of this. The Court there held that a parent did not have retained control of closely held corporation stock given in trust to his children, so as to cause the stock to be taxed in his estate, even though he retained: (1) the right to vote the actual shares given, (2) voting control over the corporation by the combined vote of these shares and other shares that he owned, (3) the right to veto any sale of the gifted shares by the trustee, and (4) the right to remove the trustee and appoint another bank in his place.

All interviewees with whom we discussed *Byrum* thought that it had exceeded their wildest expectations about the permissible limits of retained control over gifted property. "Having your cake and eating it too," was a recent description of *Byrum* in one practitioner's article.[22] Nonetheless, a series of subsequent lower court decisions

19. *See* Treas. Reg. § 25.2511-1(h)(1) (1958).

20. The theory proposed in the text has some support in the concurring opinion of Davis, J., in Chanin v. United States, 393 F.2d 972, 981 (Ct. Cl. 1968). *See also* Frank B. Thompson, 42 B.T.A. 121 (1940), *modified,* 30 A.F.T.R. 1534 (6th Cir. 1942). *But see* the majority opinion in Chanin v. United States, 393 F.2d 972 (Ct. Cl. 1968), and Robert H. Scanlon, 42 B.T.A. 997 (1941), *acq.* 1942-1 C.B. 14.

21. 408 U.S. 125 (1972).

22. Kurzman, *supra* ch. 2 note 15, at 1473.

have reinforced and even extended *Byrum*.[23] As noted above, the Tax Reform Act bars direct vote-retention and effectively overrules *Byrum* on its facts, but that statutory provision deals only with the tip of the iceberg and is easily circumvented by techniques such as those used in *Salsbury*. The new rule probably doesn't cover retained corporate control without the vote of the gift shares, nor does it do anything about the other retained powers in *Byrum*—a veto power over future sales of stock and a power to replace trustees.[24]

Byrum bespeaks a judicial attitude toward estate tax enforcement that raises doubts about the likelihood of ultimate success for any enforcement strategy that depends on changing legal rules through litigation. In particular, it casts doubt on the viability of a strategy such as that suggested above of delaying the taxability of a gift while a parent's retained control causes valuation uncertainties, since the approach would in effect circumvent the *Byrum* decision.[25]

One area where the courts might be responsive is that of valuation discounts. The valuation discount situation is such a shell game that even an unsympathetic judiciary might be convinced to cut back on it.

The Service also might expect a reasonable degree of success with steps to close off those loopholes that result from the failure to apply strictly the gift tax rules already established. Thus, we have noted that a gift is in theory made when an employer pays the premiums on group term life insurance in which all the incidents of ownership have been transferred to the employee's prospective heirs.[26] Similarly, it seems that a taxable gift may have been made at the inception of a survivorship benefit plan[27] or at the time an installment sale is entered into with an agreement to forgive unpaid installment obligations on the death of the selling parent.[28] In some of these cases the problem is largely one of discovery. Unless the Service learns of the

23. *See* Gilman v. Commissioner, 77-1 U.S. Tax Cas. ¶ 13,168 (2d Cir. 1977); Moore, *supra* ch. 2 note 10, at 442-46.

24. *See* Benjamin, *Unification and Rate Changes,* in PLI, THE TAX REFORM ACT OF 1976, 343, at 361 (1976).

25. Indeed, the Court implied that an affirmative desire not to interfere with estate-freezing strategies was the motivating force behind its decision. *See* 408 U.S. at 149 n.34.

26. *See* ch. 2 text accompanying notes 64-66 *supra*.

27. *See* ch. 2 text accompanying notes 73-74 *supra*.

28. *See* ch. 2 note 34 *supra*.

transaction within a few years of its occurrence, there is a problem in assessing a gift tax. It would seem, however, that an enterprising enforcement program might greatly increase the chances of discovery and taxation. For example, the group of taxpayers benefiting from high dollar-value, group term life insurance programs is easily identifiable in the process of income tax audits of corporations and upper-income executives. Agents might be advised to make gift tax inquiries in connection with these income tax audits.

Another situation that appears susceptible to improved enforcement and a possible toughening of legal standards is that of a sickly annuitant receiving a private annuity who dies shortly after the annuity is created.[29] These annuities will come to the attention of the Internal Revenue Service in connection with estate tax audit, and the annuity is likely to have been initiated within a few years of the annuitant's death, before the gift tax statute of limitations has expired and within the time frame of the contemplation-of-death recapture rule.[30]

Enacting New Statutory Reforms

Despite the fact that some improvement in the estate and gift tax situation might be achieved through improved enforcement, it seems unlikely that most of the problems described will respond very well to Internal Revenue Service efforts. If the estate and gift tax is to become truly effective, Congress must take steps to make it so. Congress, like the courts, traditionally has not been receptive to reinforcing the estate and gift taxes, "the neglected stepchildren of the Federal revenue system."[31] The 1976 reforms, which had been discussed for years, were enacted only as part of a statutory package that gave away much more in the form of increased exemptions than it even attempted to take back in antiavoidance measures.[32] It is somewhat puzzling why this tax, which applied only to the richest 6 percent to 7 percent of the population even before the exemption levels were raised, should have been so resistant to reform. Nonethe-

29. *See* ch. 2 text accompanying notes 84-85 *supra.*
30. *See* new I.R.C. § 2035.
31. Surrey, *supra* ch. 1 note 10, at 1.
32. *See* note 5 *supra* and source cited therein.

less, since it now applies only to some 1 percent to 2 percent of the population, the constituency directly affected by the tax has been drastically reduced. Moreover, any sympathy for poor widows or orphans who are left stranded by the death of a breadwinner seems wholly unfounded now that a widow is not even affected by the tax until her inheritance exceeds $425,000, and an orphan qualifies for a newly enacted exclusion of $5,000 times the years remaining until his or her majority[33] on top of the basic exemption of $175,000 for a single parent. For these reasons, we may be hopeful that the estate and gift tax will be more amenable to revision in the next few years than it has been in the past. The discussion below proceeds from that optimistic assumption.

In what follows, some proposals for reform or revision of the law are put forth along with thoughts and ideas on what might be considered. None of it is detailed or complete, because our own thinking on the matter has not yet evolved to that point, and because, as noted later, a reexamination of the purposes of the estate and gift tax and a consideration of alternative approaches to accomplishing those purposes should be undertaken before a final decision is made. The following discussion, then, is intended to provoke consideration of further reform rather than to determine what that reform should be, although we have some obvious biases on that question.

Taxing Wealth Already Accumulated

The highest priority must be in the area of taxing extant wealth. If an effective system cannot be devised for taxing already accumulated fortunes, there is little point in even thinking about the more sophisticated problems of estate freezing. Fortunately, there are a number of steps that can be taken to make the taxation of extant wealth significantly more effective without drastically increasing the complexity of the estate and gift tax or imposing measures of doubtful enforceability.

The first matter, which cries out for reform, is that of valuation. Since so much seems to turn on this, substantial changes in the valuation rules might be expected to accomplish much. The litigation theories proposed above for the Internal Revenue Service could easily be converted into legislative proposals and might stand a better

33. *See* new I.R.C. § 2057.

chance of success in Congress than in the courts. Thus, under the gift tax, the statute could be amended to provide that the lost value to the donor's wealth holdings, rather than any reduced value artificially generated by the donor's actions in dividing his property, should be the basis for valuation. This simple step would strike at the heart of the avoidance techniques used by Mr. Whittemore and Paulina du Pont Dean, and would seriously impair our proposed estate plan for the du Pont children. Another likely change would be to limit marketability, blockage, and cost of sale discounts, to situations where such can actually be shown to be a burden on the individuals involved.[34] In the case of minority discounts this might be accomplished by incorporating an attribution concept, such as that embodied in present section 318, into the valuation determination. It might even be desirable, and would not be unprecedented, to impose some strict limits on discounts.[35] A rigid limit would undoubtedly be opposed as unduly harsh in situations where an individual could prove that his property was subject to marketability or minority problems that reduced its value beyond the amount permitted. For such cases, the law might provide that the proceeds of an actual arm's-length sale within a reasonable period (possibly longer than the six months now provided for alternate valuation date)[36] will fix estate tax values, thus assuring that the person for whom reduced value is a liquid reality rather than a hypothetical speculation will be protected. Anyone who chooses to retain property rather than sell within the defined period could appropriately be viewed as one for whom retention value, undiminished by special discounts, rather than open-market sale value, is a more accurate measure of taxability.[37]

34. Some thought would have to be given to determining whether the situation of the recipients of property as well as the donor should be taken into account in making this assessment.

35. The Tax Reform Act provides a suggestive precedent for such limits in its treatment of private foundations. The Internal Revenue Code defines a "minimum investment return" for such a foundation as a fixed percentage (now 5%) of the market value of the foundation's assets. In making this valuation the Tax Reform Act limits discounts for blockage or the fact that securities represent ownership of a closely held corporation to 10% of the fair market value of the securities as otherwise determined. *See* new I.R.C. § 4942(e)(2). This provision also appears to impose a special burden of proof on claimants of discounts, but the draftsmanship is so poor that it is difficult to be certain.

36. *See* I.R.C. § 2032.

37. These proposals deal only with the valuation problems of discounts, leaving

The next most important reform target is the charitable front-end trust, which has a central role in structuring tax avoidance for the super rich. Restricting use of this device raises difficult questions, not as a matter of statutory drafting, but as a matter of policy.[38] There is a valuable societal by-product that results from use of these trusts and it would be foolish to think that some charitable giving might not be lost as a result of restrictions on their use. On the other hand, foreclosing these cheap charitable deductions might generate some offsetting movement toward creation of more permanent trust interests for charity, or outright gifts, especially if other avoidance avenues are foreclosed. The implications for charitable giving from limiting the use of front-end trusts are, therefore, mixed at least.

The worst abuse of the front-end trust that we have identified occurs when such a trust is funded with valuation-discounted stock in a closely held corporation because the grantor can get full tax benefit out of a cut-rate annuity based on the artificially discounted stock value. This abuse, as demonstrated in our proposed plan for the du Pont children, is so striking that it would be intolerable to allow its continuance. If the use of valuation discounts were curtailed in the manner proposed above, the concern about this particular combination would be alleviated.

Even with this extreme abuse eliminated, it would remain questionable whether the law ought to permit the continued grant of charitable deductions which, in effect, play off the income tax rates against the estate tax rates and take advantage of the fixed 6 percent discount rate built into the actuarial tables in the regulations. There is a strong argument for the position that a full charitable deduction ought not to be allowed for property that is only temporarily going to charity. An elegant solution to this problem has been suggested by Gerald Jantscher. Instead of allowing an actuarially computed de-

---

the underlying problem of determining basic asset value in its existing muddled state. Although we have no concrete proposals to advance on that matter, we might speculate that it is a problem which seems peculiarly amenable to sophisticated mathematical regression analysis as a means of at least setting outer limits on value and leavening the absurd subjectivity of such valuations with a measure of objectivity. *Cf.* Finkelstein, *Regression Models in Administrative Proceedings,* 86 HARV. L. REV. 1443 (1973) (discussing general potential for this technique as an aid to legal decisionmaking).

38. *Cf.* COMMISSION ON PRIVATE PHILANTHROPY AND PUBLIC NEEDS (FILER COMMISSION), GIVING IN AMERICA 147-51 (1975) (discussing policy considerations underlying charitable deductions for tax purposes).

duction for the future value of the charitable annuity, we might allow a full deduction for property in which a charity is given a current income interest, but require that the full value of any remaining corpus be taxed as a delayed bequest to the remaindermen at the time the property passes on to them. This proposal raises some complicated problems in implementation, but it essentially follows the pattern of the newly enacted tax on generation-skipping trusts. Various simpler, although less refined, solutions, which devalue the deduction to take account of the tax and actuarial benefits being obtained, could also be devised.

An additional reform which seems desirable to foreclose tax avoidance for the accumulated wealth of the most wealthy is some further restraint on generation-skipping and generation-jumping transfers. This could go so far as to impose a special additional tax on any transfer of property, whether outright or in trust, which effectively skips tax in one generation—for example, an outright gift of property from an individual to his grandchildren.[39] Any such transfer clearly has the result of insulating the property from tax for an extended period of time and, if the purpose of the estate tax is to assure a tax with generational periodicity, the tax is being avoided.[40] Even if this strict view is not taken, however, it seems clearly improper to permit the creation of a trust for grandchildren which is under the full control of children, including control of all investment decisions and decisions about when and how to distribute income and principal, and yet not tax that trust principal to the children's generation. The provisions of the new generation-skipping tax which permit this arrangement invite such generation-jumping avoidance.[41]

A number of other, more technical, amendments to the law are needed to prevent narrow areas of abuse which may widen over time if action is not taken. These include reforms to give the Service more power in challenging private annuities created for persons with diminished life expectancy,[42] and clarification of the treatment of outstanding installment obligations on death to foreclose the avoid-

39. *See* J. PECHMAN, FEDERAL TAX POLICY 237 (rev. ed. 1977).

40. *See* H.R. REP. No. 94-1380, 94th Cong., 2d Sess. 46-47 (1976) (suggesting goal of imposing tax with generational periodicity underlies new generation-skipping tax).

41. *See* ch. 2 text accompanying notes 127-29 *supra*.

42. *See* ch. 2 text accompanying notes 84-85 *supra*.

ance possibilities suggested by technical quirks in existing law.[43] Also, many of the problems which the Service faces in discovering transactions in time to assess a gift tax could be alleviated with a change in the statute of limitations to provide that the statute runs only as to transactions actually disclosed on a return.

These changes will foreclose most of the existing techniques for estate tax avoidance on the accumulated wealth of the very rich which are identified in this book. Two other identified problem areas with regard to accumulated wealth will remain, for which there are no easy solutions. Nothing proposed in any way prevents a wealthy person from spending money or undertaking risks on behalf of his heirs in ways which enrich the heirs at the indirect expense of the older generation. This category covers a multitude of sins (including for example the checkerboard oil deal described before) and many benign acts (such as providing an education for one's children). No simple revision of the law is going to be able to draw a neat line between sin and virtue in this area, and even if we could draw such a line, the practical difficulties of enforcing it would likely be insurmountable. However, this lacuna in the coverage of the estate and gift tax may be tolerable. Many of the grosser abuses might be addressed by better enforcement of existing law. The parent's expense of drilling in the checkerboard oil deal, for example, is vulnerable to attack under present law as a disguised gift. Moreover, the use of these spending strategies are inherently limited as an effective avoidance strategy for shifting very large amounts of wealth, because the bigger the transaction the more visible, and therefore more vulnerable, it becomes.

The other remaining problem area is use of the annual exclusion as an aggressive planning strategy. This obviously is not a matter of major interest to the very wealthy because the amounts as to which avoidance is possible are in the hundreds of thousands rather than the millions of dollars. However, it is a strategy whereby an individual with a typical family can raise the basic exempt estate to as much as a million dollars. Some may be willing to abide this, although it is presumably not the purpose for which the annual exclusion was designed. The annual exclusion makes sense as a provision which obviates the need for every person to keep track of every small intra-

43. *See* ch. 2 note 31 *supra*.

family transaction, not as an indirect means of increasing the basic exemption. No one wants to, or thinks we can, tax Christmas and birthday presents nor would it be sensible to tax amounts expended in satisfaction of normal parental obligations to provide for the support and education of children (even students beyond the legal age of majority). In practice, however, the annual exclusion is not used by tax planners to cover casual or support transactions. Instead, the working assumption seems to be that gifts of cash or liquid assets up to $6,000 (for a married taxpayer) per donee per year can be made on top of casual and support transactions, which are simply ignored.

The steps proposed by the Reporter to the American Law Institute Estate and Gift Taxation Study to alleviate this problem could be reconsidered. These are, first, to make clear that reasonable support transactions are excluded, by adopting a "transfer for consumption" exception. The annual exclusion could then be lowered to an amount which more accurately reflects normal casual gift-giving ($3,000 per year for a married taxpayer in the ALI reporter's proposal as compared to the $6,000 permitted under current law).[44] This would have the effect of halving avoidance opportunities. The ALI itself rejected this recommendation and instead proposed an overriding annual limit on use of the annual exclusion ($30,000 for a married taxpayer in the ALI recommendation).[45] This is worth considering as an alternative approach; while less drastic, it would at least put some outside curb on abuse and would put a crimp into the plans of the hypothetical millionaire who is giving $48,000 annually. It might also be conceivable to revise the exclusion to include only tangible personal property, which is the usual subject of casual gifts.

It is, however, inescapable that any reduction of the annual exclusion is going to be difficult to enforce and is going to involve tax collectors in closer scrutiny of intrafamily transactions than is necessary under existing law. The fundamental policy choices posed when one considers tampering with the annual exclusion are thus formidable and it would not be unreasonable, even though it is undesirable, to opt for a continuation of the present situation. The decision re-

44. *See* ALI, MAJOR PROBLEMS IN FEDERAL ESTATE AND GIFT TAXATION AND RECOMMENDATIONS IN REFERENCE THERETO 17-19, 39, 51 (1968).
45. *See* ALI, *supra* ch. 2 note 69, at 39, 51.

garding change in the annual exclusion ultimately must turn on the priority of goals sought by the estate and gift tax. If raising revenue is a major goal, or if mitigating modest wealth is, then the extent of avoidance through use of the annual exclusion must be very troublesome and the enforcement difficulties have to be confronted. On the other hand, if major wealth is the primary concern, then the annual exclusion situation can be viewed more complacently.

Barring the Creation of Tax-Exempt Wealth

The second major area where reform goals are clear concerns the provisions permitting creation of tax-exempt wealth. The problem of group term insurance with employer-paid premiums has already been addressed in a new ruling,[46] and that enforcement attack might be given a chance before jumping in with remedial legislation. On the legislative front, it may be repeated that a repeal of section 2039(c) is needed, although this may be a cry in the dark in view of the movement in the opposite direction in the Tax Reform Act. Finally, legislation seems needed and obtainable to deal with the growing abuse in use of survivorship benefit plans. The amounts paid to heirs under such plans are a bequest in any reasonable sense of the word and should be taxed as such. The only argument to the contrary arises when the benefit is irrevocably committed to heirs in advance of death and can be said to be a completed gift. But the employee continues to exercise inherent control in many cases by his decision whether or not to continue work and, in any event, the valuation problems are so difficult that immediate taxation as a gift is impracticable. Deferred taxation at the time of death seems the reasonable solution.[47]

Preventing Avoidance Through Estate Freezing

This brings us to the third, and most stubborn, set of avoidance issues, those we have classified as estate freezing. There are three basically different ways to address this problem: (1) take it head-on, with direct reforms, (2) give up on it, reducing even present taxation, or (3) try an end run with a fresh approach. All three must be considered serious possibilities, but none provides a sure answer.

46. *See* ch. 2 text accompanying notes 64-66 *supra.*

47. This recommendation was also made in the 1969 ALI report. *See* ALI, *supra* ch. 2 note 69, at 44, 46.

1. *Direct reforms.* The first and most natural tendency is to devise specific new provisions for the law to correct defects that have been perceived. This repairman's approach to tax reform makes sense where the fundamental structure is sound and has been taken above in formulating proposals for improving taxation of accumulated wealth and for limiting the area of tax-exempt wealth. Turning to estate freezing, however, the case for reformist repairs is at best uneasy.

The problems posed in formulating direct reforms to restrict estate freezing activity become evident when a possible response is considered to the *Salsbury*-type recapitalization, which we have discussed as a model of estate freezing strategy. There are four separate transfer tax problems raised by the *Salsbury*-type recapitalization. First, there is the tax-free shift of future growth, which is inherent in any gift. Second, there is the effective way in which this future growth has been separated from present value through the dual-stock structure to maximize tax avoidance. Third, there is the retained enjoyment and control held by the donor parent through his continued ownership of the majority of voting stock. And, fourth, there is the continuing parental contribution to the growth and development of the corporation which is indirectly diverted to the next generation free of tax.

The most obvious locus for reform is the third aspect (retained rights). The Code has long recognized the tax avoidance implications of transfers with retained rights in sections 2036 and 2038, and has dealt with these problems by recapturing the property for purposes of estate taxation, that is, treating it as if it had never been transferred. Congress could consider attacking the *Salsbury* transaction with amendments to sections 2036 and 2038 which expand the definitions of retained income and control needed to invoke those provisions. As the Supreme Court dryly observed in one of its more enlightened moments, the transfer of corporate property by an individual who retains voting control over the corporation "may properly be said to have left him with more than a memory" of the property.[48] Whether Congress should go so far as to adopt a statutory standard of total amnesia may be questioned. But there is little doubt that the modest anti-*Byrum* provision in the Tax Reform Act does little to

48. Commissioner v. Sunnen, 333 U.S. 591, 608 (1947).

prevent a transferor from effectively retaining control over corporate property in which an interest has been transferred. To be fair and effective any modification of the law to deal with this problem must not only be phrased more broadly than the anti-*Byrum* rule but must also cover partnership arrangements. We observed earlier[49] that limited partnerships, particularly with structured interests, have an unexploited potential that surely would be developed if the corporate rules were tightened.

All these objectives could be accomplished by an amendment to section 2038 providing that the power to manage or to select the management of a corporation, partnership, or other business entity, by exercise of voting rights, contract rights or otherwise, will be considered a power to alter or amend the beneficial enjoyment of all ownership interests in the entity. This could be viewed more as a clarification of the principle in the existing statute than a revision of it and might not even have required a statutory amendment if the present rules had been interpreted in the manner urged by the government in *Byrum*.[50]

Such changes in sections 2036 and 2038 would not, however, really accomplish very much to block the *Salsbury* transaction because the way would remain open to achieve the same ends through the mechanism of a sale rather than a gift. The present rules exempt any "bona fide sale for an adequate and full consideration." A corporation can be established with the dual-stock structure, and the

49. *See* ch. 2 text accompanying notes 36-43 *supra*.

50. *See* 408 U.S. at 132 n.4. *See also* 408 U.S. at 151-68 (White, J., dissenting). This proposed rule leaves open the question of how to treat retained investment and other administrative powers as trustee of property transferred to a trust. Such powers do not give rise to recapture under present law so long as limited by fiduciary obligations. Old Colony Trust Co. v. United States, 423 F.2d 601 (1st Cir. 1970). However, because this invites estate-freezing diversions of parental abilities to children, a return to the contrary *State Street Trust* rule might be more in keeping with the purposes of the statute. State Street Trust Co. v. United States, 263 F.2d 635 (1st Cir. 1959). Nonetheless, the trust situation may be distinguished on the ground that the fiduciary obligations of a trustee are so much more well defined and readily enforceable than the rather amorphous fiduciary duty which a controlling shareholder owes to minority shareholders. *See* Brief for United States at 14-21, United States v. Byrum, 408 U.S. 125 (1972). To the extent a trust instrument widens trustee powers and dilutes common law trustee obligations, the situation may begin to resemble that in a corporation or partnership, and the basis for different treatment vanishes. *See* R. STEPHENS, G. MAXFIELD, S. LIND, FEDERAL ESTATE AND GIFT TAXATION 4-126 to 4-129 (3d ed. 1974).

low-value common stock can be sold to the children for adequate and full consideration (which would be nominal given the nominal value of the stock) rather than given to them, thereby completely removing it from the net of sections 2036 and 2038. Indeed, this is only one striking example of the way in which a "sale" of property with retained income or control can effectively be used to make sections 2036 and 2038 meaningless. This sale technique, especially when coupled with well-planned use of installment payments, poses a grave threat to the integrity of the basic principle embodied in sections 2036 and 2038. Why should the taxpayer make an immediate gift with retained income or control, and be subject to sections 2036 and 2038, when he can make an installment sale to children with retained income and control, subsequently give the property away to the children through forgiveness of the installment payments, and entirely avoid section 2036 and 2038?[51] To combat this, sections 2036 and 2038 might be amended to cover sales to family members, where a parent retains a defined interest in property. The theory of excluding sales from the scope of sections 2036 and 2038 is presumably that when property is sold the selling parent's estate is not depleted but rather resupplied with equivalent value property. This theory, however, fails to take account of future growth opportunities which are shifted on the sale. Since the shift of this future growth with retained income and control is such an important part of estate tax avoidance, an expansion of sections 2036 and 2038 to cover family sales with retained interests seems essential if we are going to take meaningful action against *Salsbury*-type transactions.

The difficulties in writing this new provision should not be underestimated. There is first the problem of determining how much, if any, credit should be given a purchasing child for his contributions to the future growth and development of the property, especially in a case like *Salsbury* where the child has participated actively for a substantial period. However, under present law we give no credit for this in the case of gift property recaptured under sections 2036 and 2038, and arguably the problem is so intractable that we have no

51. If, and probably only if, the property involved has unrealized appreciation, the question in the text is not entirely rhetorical, since the sale as distinguished from a gift would generate a possible capital gains tax. This tax may be avoidable, however. *See* ch. 2 text accompanying notes 30-34 *supra*. Moreover, the new carryover basis rule makes payment of this capital gains tax a less severe burden than in the past.

choice but to follow the same route in sale cases. This would mean that a parent would have to cut all control strings if he wished to avoid risk of having a donee's efforts reflected in the parent's own estate. In other words, it would be difficult for a parent who wished to maintain ongoing dominance of a family business to shift a part of the future growth of that business to a child, even if the child is active in the business and pays for a share in it. That may seem harsh, but it is simply a reflection of the significance of continued dominance. If the parent will not let go of control, the law is justified in treating that control as significant. Moreover, unless we go this far it is doubtful that we will have put any severe dent into the plans of future Salsburys.

Consideration will also have to be given to defining the specific family grouping which would invoke this "sale" recapture rule. However, it might be better to address the matter with a more general definition focusing on the donative coloration which is so likely in an intrafamily sale. In addition to avoiding the difficulties of drawing a fine line among various family relations, this more general definitional approach would also leave the way open for some sales to children to escape the rule if truly bona fide and arm's length. These objectives could be accomplished by rewriting the present bona fide sale exception in the statute to cover only "a bona fide transfer made in the ordinary course of business and without any significant donative purpose." A caveat might be added in the statute or its legislative history that a sale to specified family members (lineal descendants of the transferor's parents?) will be presumed, subject to rebuttal, to have this donative purpose.[52] Such a statutory change, while here again more a change of spirit than the introduction of a new basic principle, could be expected to reverse the existing tendency of the courts to treat transactions such as that in *Hudspeth* so leniently.[53]

---

52. For a similar recommendation, see ALI, *supra* ch. 2 note 69, at 157.

53. Provision would, of course, have to be made to offset the amount paid on sale to prevent double counting. At the minimum, the fair market value (at the time of payment) of the consideration paid would have to be deducted from the estate. Beyond that some account might be taken of the fact that this consideration itself has been subject to appreciation. Tracing seems impractical, but an adjustment might be considered for the general rate of inflation between the date of sale and the date of taxation. In cases like *Hudspeth*, where no payment is actually made, each being forgiven as it comes due, it is questionable whether any offset should be allowed.

If sections 2036 and 2038 are amended to cover sales with retained income and control as suggested, the installment sale technique as employed in *Hudspeth,* where the parent leased the property back, and like cases where ownership rights are effectively retained, should no longer pose a serious estate tax avoidance problem. The way would nonetheless remain open for use of the installment sale technique in situations where the parent retains no income or control interest in the property within the meaning of the statutory provisions. Thus, for instance, a parent who held valuable property which he expected to appreciate rapidly could sell the property to his children promptly in an installment sale and then give the property to them by piecemeal forgiving of installment obligations. He would thus gain all the estate-freezing benefit of an immediate gratuitous transfer even though the transfer is in reality spread out over many years. If this is thought to be a serious problem it could be dealt with in a statutory amendment which defined certain retained rights to installment payments from property in intrafamily sales as being the equivalent of retained income, although the likelihood of such statute penalizing bona fide intrafamily installment sales would have to be given serious consideration. An alternative might be simply to bar use of the annual exclusion in cases where installment payments are forgiven.

Even if all of this were done, Congress still would have prevented only use of the estate-freezing technique with regard to transfers of future growth in property already owned. Thus, the way would remain open to divert new business and investment opportunities to children, including situations in which the parent controls the new opportunity, without incurring any estate or gift tax. For example, the arrangement described earlier whereby a new corporation partially owned by children but controlled by parents is created to market new products of a family business[54] could continue to be fully effective in accomplishing estate planning goals. So, too, would similar arrangements in partnership structures or in deals dominated by parents. There simply is no "transfer with retained interest" in such cases, because the older generation never owned the interest acquired by the younger. In an attempt to deal with this, sections 2036 and 2038 could be further amended to cover all property in

54. *See* ch. 2 text accompanying notes 17-18 *supra.*

which the older generation has a controlling interest or over which it exercises management control, even if the older generation never actually owned the property. However, such a provision carries the risk that, while blocking areas of abuse, it is also likely to discourage many parent-child cooperative ventures which wise public policy might wish to stimulate. A resolution of this dilemma, while not out of the question, certainly would pose a major challenge for the skilled draftsman.

If all these proposed amendments were enacted, they would not fully terminate estate-freezing opportunities. There would remain many avoidance possibilities through intrafamily fringe benefits and diversions which seem beyond the reach of any plausible statute. That is not to say that some of these intrafamily fringe benefits could not be attacked, but it is unlikely that a comprehensive statute taxing such benefits can be written or that anyone would want to live in the society that has such a law if it were enacted. The frustrating problems which the Internal Revenue Service has confronted in attempting to define which employer fringe benefits are taxable under the income tax law gives warning of the difficulties of writing a truly complete transfer tax law. In addition, and perhaps most significant, none of these recommendations would do anything about the estate-freezing benefits of simple, straightforward gifts of property without retained control, even though that may well be a much more important avoidance area for the very wealthy than retained control situations.

The unfortunate conclusion to be drawn from all of this is that, while it is possible to tax many instances of estate freezing, not all such activity can be covered. Each step toward improving the effectiveness of the transfer tax in this area can have unintended effects impinging upon family relationships. Even if one could be cavalier about these side effects, it is impossible to blink the fact that political resistance to much expansion of sections 2036 and 2038 in this direction will be severe and the resisters will have cogent arguments to offer.

This presents a classic tax-policy dilemma. Which is better, to tax some items when functionally similar items cannot be covered, or to forsake taxing the entire class of items? Either result is second best. On some occasions when this dilemma is posed the uncovered segment may be reduced sufficiently to give confidence that the equity and neutrality problems are not too severe, and that the fundamental policy being implemented is not negated. That was our tentative conclusion in discussing reform of the taxation of extant wealth. There, an area of untaxed indirect transfers was seen to remain even if all our proposed reforms were adopted, but that residual area seemed tolerable. The residuum in the estate-freezing area is more problematic. It is most probable, given the problems in designing reasonable legislative reforms to cope with estate freezing, that taxpayers who wish to shift and divert future growth will remain able to do so to a substantial extent.

In addition, there is a danger that reform will create new traps for the unwary and penalize the group of taxpayers who for personal or technical reasons find themselves unable to take advantage of avoidance avenues—in other words, will recreate some of the problems we are seeking to eliminate. For example, a skeptic may correctly ask if there was any real point to the anti-*Byrum* provision included in the Tax Reform Act of 1976. This provision closed off a clear area of abuse when it prevented individuals from retaining the vote in corporate stock while claiming to have shifted it to heirs for estate tax purposes, but the way remains open to accomplish the same ends so easily that we have more likely entrapped those who retain the actual vote than prevented any purposeful avoidance. In such circumstances a little reform may be worse than none at all.

This reasoning does not mean that a policy of benign neglect is necessarily the correct approach to the matter of estate freezing. Even under existing law, due primarily to the effects of the existing recapture provisions, some kinds of estate freezing are successful and others not. Moreover, the existing rules under sections 2036 and 2038 and allied provisions are well known to be a morass which includes many doubtful situations along with the deserved. With the changes made in estate and gift taxation in 1976, a complete reassessment and revision of these recapture rules is now overdue. Some expansion of the definitions in these provisions in the direction suggested may be desirable to reduce unintended equity and neutrality misfortunes and to accomplish more properly the goal of limiting erosions of the tax base. On the other hand, this review may lead to the conclusion that the present rules are overdrawn in some respects and create unwarranted traps. To the extent we revise these rules, we should be prepared to reform in the direction of reduced as well as increased coverage. Less is sometimes more in the art of taxation, as elsewhere.[55]

2. *Reducing present taxation.* An extreme version of reduced coverage has been proposed as a solution to this entire problem by the American Law Institute. The Institute proposed that when the estate and gift taxes were combined (as is now the case), an easy-to-complete-gift rule should be adopted.[56] Only if a donor of property retained the beneficial enjoyment of it (ordinarily speaking, the income) or held the full power to revest the donated property in himself would the property be recaptured for his estate. This would essentially give carte blanche to estate freezers, as the Institute's report acknowledged: "It would allow a transferor to retain many strings on a transfer and nevertheless get the value of the future growth out from under transfer taxation, as long as the strings do not permit the transferor to pull the property back to himself."[57] What is more:

The easy-to-complete-gift policy that is possible under a unified tax is regarded by some as one of the most attractive features of such a tax. The vote of the Tax Advisory Group at the May 1967 meeting was forty-three to two in favor of an easy-to-complete-gift rule if a unified transfer tax is adopted.[58]

Undoubtedly, this enthusiasm was provoked by the simplifying aspects of an easy-to-complete-gift rule, but the estate tax implications give reason for pause. The ALI proposal emphasizes retained income and revocability as the only forbidden conditions. No one would challenge the significance of revocability. However, some might feel that a retained power to control the ultimate recipient of property, which would be ignored under the ALI rule, is even more significant than retained income. For a very wealthy person, who has more income than he can consume currently, the real deterrent to gift-giving may be the unwillingness to guarantee an inheritance to a particular person and thereby surrender power and influence over

55. For some discussion of alternatives for modifying present recapture rules, *see* ALI, *supra* ch. 2 note 69, at 188-98.
56. *Id.* at 41-43, 46.
57. *Id.* at 42.
58. *Id.*

that person. For such a wealth holder, the opportunity to gain estate-freezing benefits while putting property in an accumulating trust with reserved power to appoint the trust property to anyone except himself, and with reserved trust powers to control trust investments, all of which would be permitted under the ALI rule,[59] may be as appealing as the briar patch was to B'rer Rabbit. To guard against this, it is necessary to modify the ALI proposal to require that a donor seeking to avoid recapture make fixed and final designation of the beneficiaries of his gift (by name or by formula) or at least release all major powers to control selection of beneficiaries, even though this would sacrifice much of the desired simplicity of the easy gift rule.

It is also questionable whether retained income should trigger recapture. Once a future interest is irrevocably committed to particular beneficiaries, the donor has sacrificed his testamentary power over the property. Why should not that be the critical date for taxation if gifts are to be easy to make? No reason or justification is given in the ALI report other than to observe that the proposed rule would permit transfers with retained income to be made "without the transferor diminishing his holdings by payment of a transfer tax at the time the arrangement is established."[60] True, but why is this important?

The ALI report does not grapple with these questions because it proceeds from the convenient assumption that they are not really very important once the estate and gift tax is unified with a single rate scale. This assumption, however, ignores the continued rate advantage for gifts stemming from the failure to include the tax on the gift tax base.[61] More significantly, it brushes aside estate freezing as if it were not even an issue. For those who concur in the ALI assumption, the solution to the estate freezing problem is easy—ignore it. But for those who are bothered by the *Salsbury* case and the other examples of estate freezing discussed in this book, this assumption does not seem very realistic, and the easy-to-complete-gift approach is disturbingly inadequate.

59. *Id.* at 191.

60. *Id.* at 43.

61. The ALI report did call for correction of this rate advantage as to gifts made in "two taxable periods" prior to death. *Id.* at 118. The Tax Reform Act has a similar, but broader, rule covering all gifts within three years of death. *See* new I.R.C. § 2035. The failure to gross-up gifts made earlier is usually justified as a fair trade-off for the earlier payment of tax in such cases. *See* ALI, *supra* ch. 2 note 69, at 190. But this analysis ignores estate freezing, as noted in the text.

3. *A fresh approach.* Neither the direct-reform approach nor the easy-to-complete-gift approach seems to offer an ultimate solution to the basic problem of estate freezing—distinguishing those situations where post-gift appreciation should continue to be taxed to the donor from those situations where it should not be. This difficulty may only lie in the practical problems of drafting and enforcement, but it may go deeper. It may be that there is simply no strong underlying policy for drawing sharp distinctions in this area. What purpose is served by having major tax burdens turn on when and how property is transferred?

If we define the purpose of the estate and gift tax as imposing a levy on the value of all property at the time the property is transferred, the question is of course circular, and it answers itself. However, that seems an odd way to state the purpose of the tax. The purpose of the transfer tax is no more to tax transfers than the purpose of the income tax is to tax income. This is rather only a description of the tax base. Its purpose must be found in its economic or social goals. In the case of the estate tax, it is difficult to find a consensus on these goals. The historical record indicates that the estate and gift tax was originally intended to serve as a revenue producer.[62] This most likely is at least a part of its purpose today,[63] although some would disagree.[64] In addition, a variety of social goals are stated for the tax:[65] supplementing the income tax, breaking up large fortunes, and preventing the creation of a coupon-clipper class. All of these purposes or goals might better be served by an annual or a periodic wealth tax[66] than by the estate and gift taxes.

From a revenue viewpoint, a wealth tax is clearly superior to an estate and gift tax. The wealth tax base is not eroded by post-gift appreciation, since wealth in the hands of transferees would continue to be subject to taxation when the next tax period rolled around, rather than shifted out of the clutches of the tax for a generation. This

62. *See* Eisenstein, *The Rise and Decline of the Estate Tax,* 11 TAX L. REV. 223, 223-52 (1955).

63. ALI, *supra* ch. 2 note 69, at 49-50.

64. *Hearings, supra* Intro. note 1, at 1210 (statement of Richard B. Covey).

65. *See* sources cited in ch. 1 notes 8-10 *supra.*

66. Such a tax, which would be a "property tax" on personal property as well as real property with an offset for indebtedness, is a standard part of European tax systems. *See* C. SANDFORD, J. WILLIS & D. IRONSIDE, AN ANNUAL WEALTH TAX, app. C. (1975) (tabular summary of existing European wealth taxes).

simple fact means that the significance of estate freezing as an avoidance technique would be sharply diminished. (This is not to say that
tax revenues might not continue to be affected by intergenerational
transfers. Assuming that the wealth tax had progressive rates and
was imposed on individuals, rather than family groupings, a transfer
of some wealth to a poorer taxpayer would reduce tax collections by
reducing the tax bracket, but it could not completely remove property from the tax base. Moreover, the value of intergenerational
transfers as a tax avoidance technique would be inherently self-
limiting because the more that was given to a person the closer his
tax bracket would move to that of the donor. Assuming that a flat
top rate would come into effect at some level, the super rich would
soon hit that level and thereby have exhausted the tax avoidance
opportunities in bracket-lowering transfers.)

As a supplement to the income tax, the wealth tax seems preferable to transfer taxation. The primary goal in this respect is to take
account of the fact that the existing income tax underrates accumulated wealth as a source of ability to pay because it reaches only the
net realized returns on capital; all the indirect benefits of wealth—
power, security, appreciation—must be reached by some other tax,
if at all.[67] Another asserted income tax supplementary goal is adding
to the progressivity of the overall tax system. While the estate and gift
tax serves both these goals, it does so only erratically; the wealth tax
would do it more consistently and more evenhandedly. The wealth
tax is also far superior in attacking large fortunes because it does so
regularly and promptly and cannot be evaded through generational
shifting of ownership.

The choice of taxes is not quite so easy when we turn to the goal of
preventing coupon clippers, because the wealth tax strikes all wealth
holders equally, whether they created their fortunes or were given
them. However, a major point of this book is that much of the growth

67. Not everyone agrees, of course, that wealth is undertaxed. It is possible to
conclude that quite the opposite is true. *See Hearings Before the House Ways and
Means Comm. on Tax Reform,* 94th Cong., 1st Sess., pt. 1, at 1, 17-18 (1975)
(statement of Hon. William E. Simon). The resolution of this dispute depends to a
great extent on the questions one is asking. (What exactly is undertaxed relative to
what: property income compared to labor income, or saving compared to consumption? What is the criterion of undertaxation: equity, or economic efficiency?) This
is part of the legal and economic analysis which must precede any serious development of a wealth tax for the United States. *See* note 69 *infra.*

of property in the hands of a wealthy person is attributable to his or her parents or the result of his or her having been given capital. To the extent that property growth is derived from such sources, the wealth tax is a superior means of taxing the idle rich. (In other words, the wealth tax addresses the problem we have referred to as infra-family fringe benefits.) On the other hand, to the extent that the wealth tax sweeps in self-produced wealth, it can be viewed as inferior.

One other major advantage of the periodic wealth tax should also be mentioned. It has always been difficult for people to accept the idea of having a large chunk of property seized by the government in one fell swoop, particularly when the property is in an illiquid form and payment of the tax may require disposition of some or all of it. This in large part explains why Congress has consistently been sympathetic to mitigating the estate tax payment of farmers and small businessmen and why the courts have been so sympathetic to valuation discounts for closely held stock. The result of this understandable sympathy has been a substantial complication of the estate tax and an erosion of its base.

This problem could be eliminated under a periodic wealth tax. Because such a tax would be imposed much more frequently than an estate tax, it could carry correspondingly lower rates than the existing scale for estate and gift taxes. For example, an annual net wealth tax with a flat rate of 1 percent imposed only on net wealth in excess of $200,000 (thus limiting the tax to only the richest 1 percent to 2 percent of the population and even for them exempting the first $200,000) would have produced approximately the same revenue in 1972 as did the estate and gift tax in that year.[68] Given the greatly increased exemption levels and consequent lowered revenue estimates for the post-1976 estate and gift tax, it is probable that this

68. This admittedly rough revenue estimate for a 1% wealth tax is derived as follows. All data is from *Hearings, supra* Intro. note 1, at 1311 (statement of Prof. James D. Smith). As of 1972, the top 1% to 1.5% of wealthholders had net worths in excess of $200,000 (*id.* at 1313). The 2,090,000 persons in this group had an aggregate net worth of $915.9 billion (*id.* at 1317). Subtracting $200,000 per person to allow for a basic exemption, the remaining tax base is $497.9 billion. A 1% tax on this base yields $4.979 billion, compared to the $5.436 billion produced by the estate and gift tax in that year. This was an aberrationally good year for the estate and gift tax, the best ever in its history. In 1971 it produced only $3.7 billion and in 1973 only $4.9 billion. Even in 1976, the next best year, the collections were only $5.2 billion.

hypothetical 1 percent net wealth tax on top wealth holders would be a better revenue producer than the new estate and gift tax, as well as being superior for the other reasons discussed above. Such a 1 percent tax would of course be far easier on holders of nonliquid assets than the existing high rate estate and gift tax.

This is, of course, only a brief look at the periodic wealth tax. A fuller evaluation requires a more careful articulation of the goals of taxation in this area and a careful choice among those goals. Unfortunately, and perhaps surprisingly, that evaluation cannot be undertaken easily because these goals have never been thought through in any coherent way. The goals discussed above have grown up more as slogans than rationally developed policies. Until the quality of this underlying analysis is improved and the role of estate and gift taxation in our overall tax structure is clarified, no solid conclusion can be reached regarding the ultimate merits of different approaches to taxation in this area.

Moreover, even apart from this lack of clarity as to underlying goals, there is not space here to undertake an extended discussion of the periodic net wealth tax which, of course, has a number of special practical and legal problems of its own.[69] This is simply the place to observe that such a tax or some variation on the theme has much to be said for it, and that a large part of the dissatisfaction with the treatment of estate freezing under the estate and gift tax is the result of a tendency to want it to do what a net wealth tax can do and to be disturbed because the sow's ear is not better at tapping silk purses.

For the time being, there are a number of steps, which have been described above, that can reasonably be taken to improve the estate and gift tax. Those measures, in particular the modifications in valuation procedures to stop the absurd abuses now occurring, will do much to protect the tax base and improve the fairness and effective-

---

69. To list the more serious problems in no particular order, there are (1) the practical difficulties of periodic valuation, (2) the constitutional problem of imposing a direct tax not apportioned according to population, (3) the practical and privacy implications of requiring a full reporting of wealth holdings, and (4) the economic implications of taxing capital as distinguished from income. The tendency in the United States has been to dismiss the wealth tax out-of-hand because of this set of problems, but the time may be ripe to think more seriously about it here. *See* J. Pechman, *supra* note 39, at 242-43; C. Sandford, J. Willis, & D. Ironside, *supra* note 66; Thurow, *Net Worth Taxes,* 25 Nat'l Tax J. 417 (1972). The text by C. Sandford, et al., includes a useful bibliography at 337-38.

ness of the tax in reaching existing accumulated wealth. As for estate freezing, some improvements in sections 2036 and 2038 can raise the ante substantially for taxpayers who want to transfer future growth to their prospective heirs and thereby can limit the greatest abuses in this area. But a periodic wealth tax suggests itself as a theoretically superior long-run solution to this problem.[70]

70. For a detailed discussion of the potential for an American wealth tax, *see* Cooper, *Taking Wealth Taxation Seriously,* 33 THE RECORD OF THE ASS'N OF THE BAR OF THE CITY OF NEW YORK, January 1979.

Index